UBÏQ: A MENTAL ODYSSEY

MATHIEU BRIAND & DANIEL FOUCARD

ENCOUNTERS

UBÏQ: A MENTAL ODYSSEY

in Memorium of Albert Hofmann

If you draw a dot in a space you define one space.
If you draw another dot and you join it to the first you define a line.
If you draw a third dot and you join that to the other two you define a two-dimensional space.
If you draw a fourth dot outside or inside the triangle and you join that to the three previous dots you form a three-dimensional space.

The Psychodrhomme in "Mental Shift", chap 1, (1623)

If you draw a circle in the sand and study only what's inside the circle, then that is a closed-system perspective. If you study what is inside the circle and everything outside the circle, then that is an open system perspective.

Buckminster Fuller

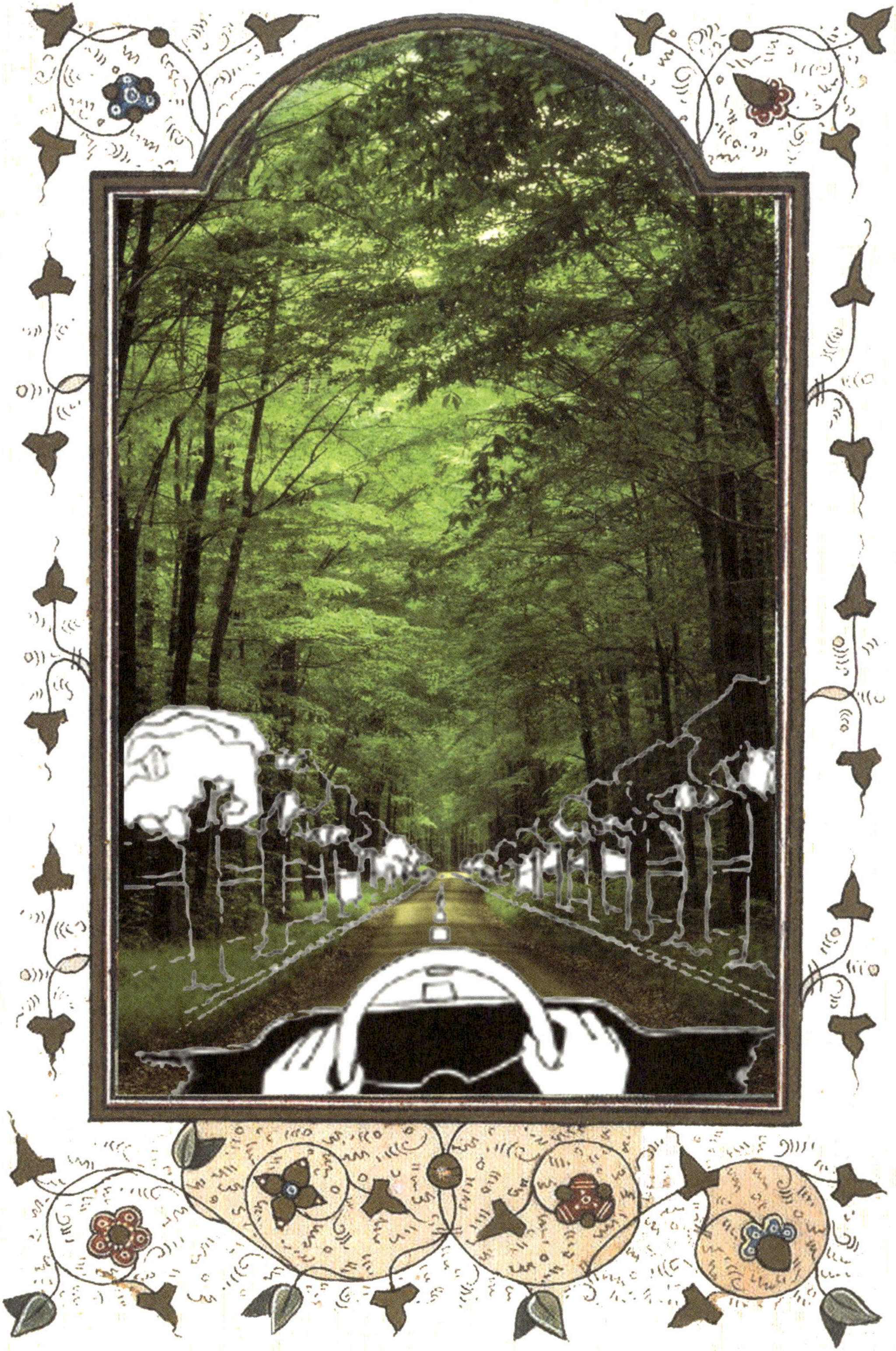

To Caroline

You will remain forever in our hearts.
We were not ready for that confrontation.
We will be forever traumatized.
The Psychotière has set its circular trap, an endless torture race to try to reach one another.
The infinite loop can only be neutralized through inserting and shifting a third dot.

7TH FEBRUARY 1804
LOGBOOK OF THE FIRST MATE

The Reign

Exhausted still after the heavy fight against Lenson's elusive frigate, we saw a strange vessel approaching. It too seemed to have fought a battle in which it had lost its three masts, for the dark mass was moving by itself, with no sails, no masts, no rudder. Our captain hesitated for a while before firing a volley. No flag, no distress signal, a name impossible to make out. It passed thirty feet from our ship, and we could see that our two boats had been conceived on an almost identical model. It was empty and we looked in vain, leaning over uneasily, for any battle traces still visible on the deck. We thought its crew had abandoned ship in a hurry. We boarded it. The atmosphere was overwhelmingly calm. No objects in sight, no damage either. There are thousands of reasons for abandoning ship in mid-course, but having forgotten to fix masts bearing sails implied that no crew had ever set foot on it. We searched the store rooms for riches, some traces of activity, some spare sails: there was nothing. Except for a book, written in a foreign language, a precious piece of writing which would tell us a bit more about that vessel, but not a single well-read man on board managed to decipher it.

D R E A M

12:25 GMT

SECRET SIDE

COPWAY SPACESHIP ORG

THE IMAGE WE ARE GOING TO COMMENT ON HAS BEEN COMMUNICATED TO THE FEDERAL AUTHORITIES FOR AN ACTIVE RESEARCH PROGRAM. THE SHIP OUR SATELLITE 5 HAS CLEARLY IDENTIFIED AS DRIFTING NW/EW IS A THREE-DECK VESSEL RESEMBLING THOSE USED BY THE BRITISH NAVY AROUND 1820. WITH NO MASTS, BUT WITH AN INTACT FLOATING STRUCTURE, IT COULD BE ONE OF THOSE CURIOSITIES RESISTING MARINE EROSION REPORTED BY NUMEROUS NAVIGATORS. AFTER SOME RESEARCH ON RELIABLE DATA, THE PREVIOUS DESCRIPTION OF AN ABANDONED SHIP DATING FROM THE SAME ERA GOES BACK TO 1905. THE CAPTAIN OF A TRAWLER FROM JAMESTOWN STATED AT THE TIME HAVING BRUSHED AGAINST A VESSEL IN EXCELLENT CONDITION DATING FROM THE PIRATE ERA. IT SEEMED ABSURD THAT SUCH A SHIP COULD KEEP AFLOAT FOR ALMOST A CENTURY ON THE ATLANTIC OCEAN.

HOWEVER, THE SAILOR'S DESCRIPTION WAS CONSISTENT WITH THE MARINE ENGINEERING OF A THREE-DECK VESSEL. A FRUITLESS SEARCH TO FIND IT ENSUED. THE VESSEL WE HAVE ON THAT PICTURE PRESENTS TO THE METER CHARACTERISTICS SIMILAR TO THOSE OF THE TESTIMONY. THE IMAGE ENABLES US TO SEE A SOMEWHAT IMPECCABLE DECK THAT DOESN'T APPEAR TO HAVE BEEN SWEPT BY WAVES, WIND OR STORM. THE WHOLE THING RESEMBLES A GIANT FLOATING BOAT THAT HAS JUST SLID DOWN ITS SLIPWAY. A FEW OBJECTS ARE VISIBLE, AMONGST THEM A BOOK, A TRIANGULAR CONTAINER, A BARREL AND ITS HOOPING STACKED ON THE SIDE.

DR E A M

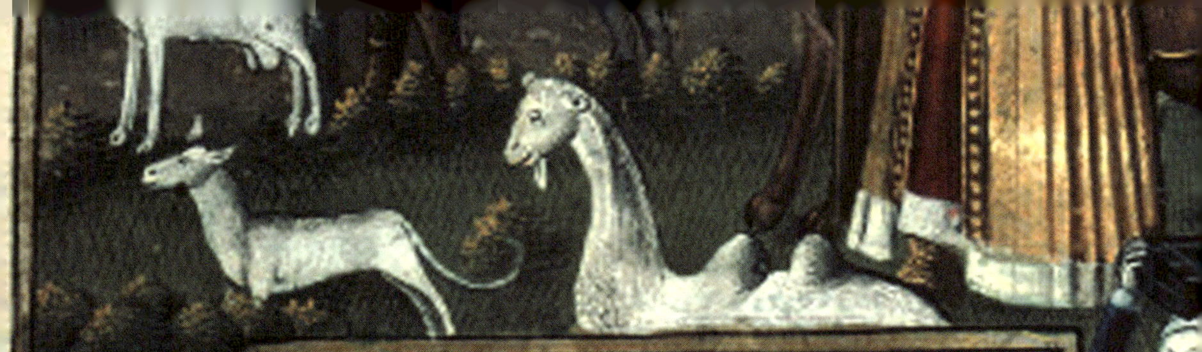

We arrive at the Feast.

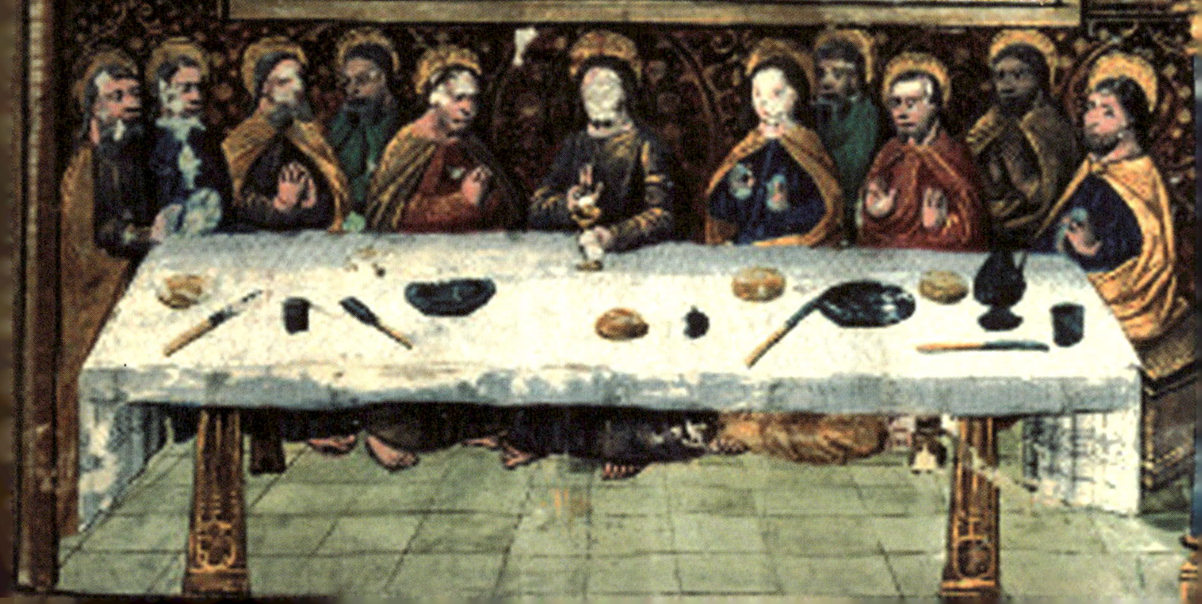

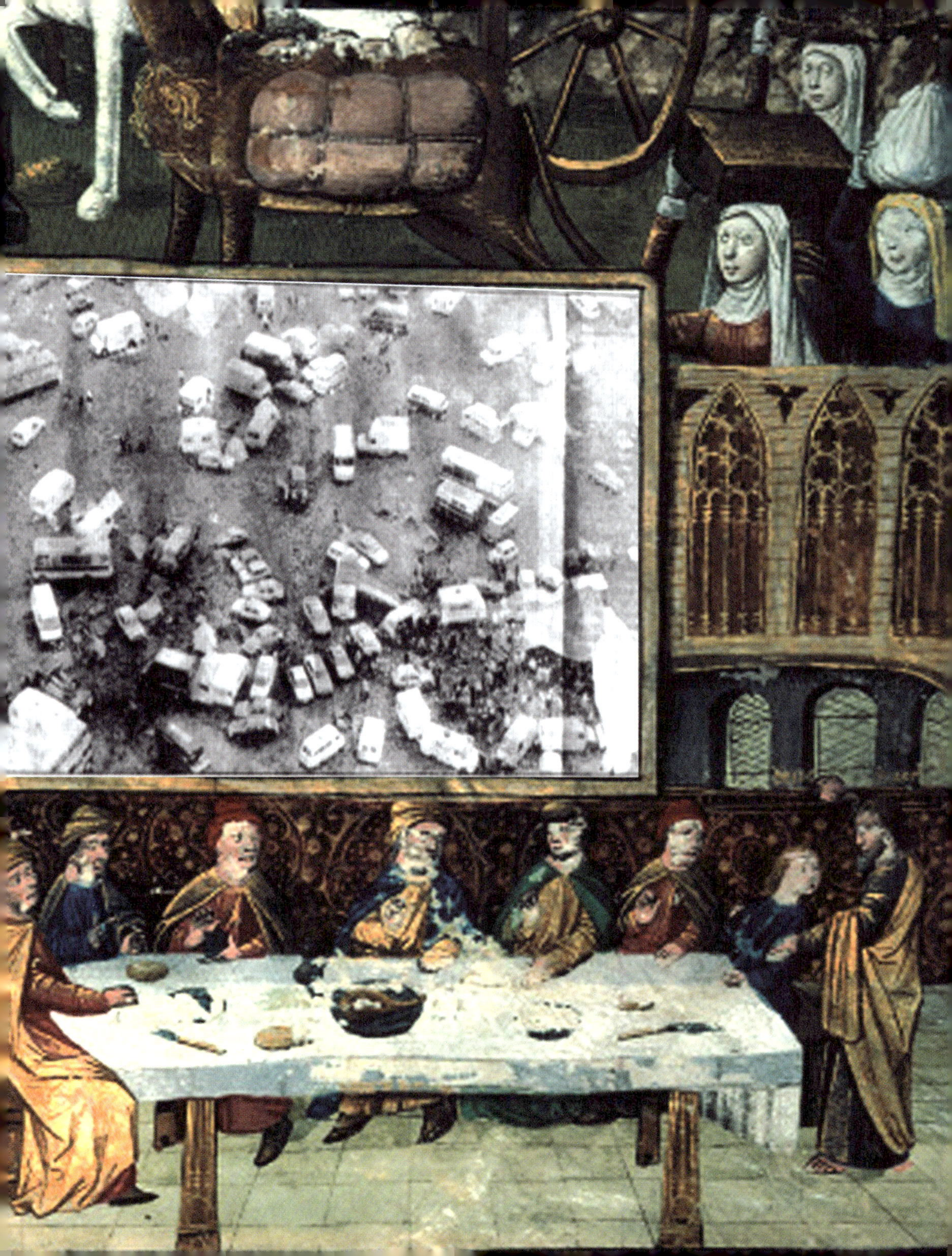

Dishevelled punk
in the starry night
Electricity pirate
You unload your enormous sound
In strange hypnotic loops.

725
OFF CRETE
ORIONTE

THE BYZANTINE HISTORIAN ORIONTE TELLS OF THE STRANGE ENCOUNTER MADE BY AN ESCORT ACCOMPANYING A TRANSPORT OF SPICES NEAR THE CRETAN COAST WHEN THE CONVOY WAS GOING BACK TO BYZANTIUM. THE ESCORT WAS IN THE HANDS OF A FAMOUS SAILOR WHO'D HAD THE IDEA OF MULTI-DIRECTIONAL SHOOTING BY PLACING SEVERAL MUZZLES OF GREEK FIRE AT THE EXTREMITIES OF A DROMOND WHOSE CONSTRUCTION HE HAD SUPERVISED. THE DROMOND IS A POWERFUL BYZANTINE VESSEL, A REPLICA OF THE GREEK TRIREME, FURNISHED WITH A HUNDRED OARS, EACH SIDE WITH FIFTY ROWERS ON TWO LEVELS. BUT IT IS BETTER KNOWN FOR ITS GREEK FIRE, AN INCENDIARY MIXTURE WITH A MINERAL OIL BASE, THAT IS BROUGHT TO THE SHIP'S PROW BY A TUBE IN A LION'S MOUTH THAT SPITS FLAMES DURING BATTLE. THAT SAILOR IMAGINED AN INTERLACED DESIGN OF TUBES, MAKING IT POSSIBLE TO FIRE ALSO FROM THE SIDES, GIVING IT THE ADVANTAGE OF BEING ABLE TO ESCORT SEVERAL COMMERCIAL SHIPS THANKS TO ITS FIERCE REPUTATION. THUS, WHEN AN ENORMOUS VESSEL WITH NO MASTS AGGRESSIVELY APPROACHED THE DROMOND, THE SAILOR OPENED FIRE. THE INCENDIARY MIXTURE HAD NO EFFECT WHATSOEVER ON THE STRUCTURE IN BRACKISH WOOD DRIFTING WITHOUT A CREW, BUT THE MAIN THING WAS THAT THE ESCORT KEPT GOING WITHOUT ANY PROBLEM. RETURNING TO HARBOUR, THE SAILOR BECAME A TALENTED STORY TELLER; HE TALKED ABOUT THE FLOATING ISLAND, THE ROMAN SKIFF, THE ARCH.

D R E A M

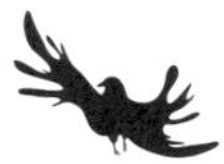

The free party is in sight.
Park your VW there.
Here are the doses.
What's that?
Phials.
How did you get that stuff?
A pharmaceutical lab supplies the vets, or so it seems.
How do you take it?
You never used a phial? You break the tips, and you pour it down. Trip guaranteed.
Give me two or three, then.
No, one will be enough, you'll see.

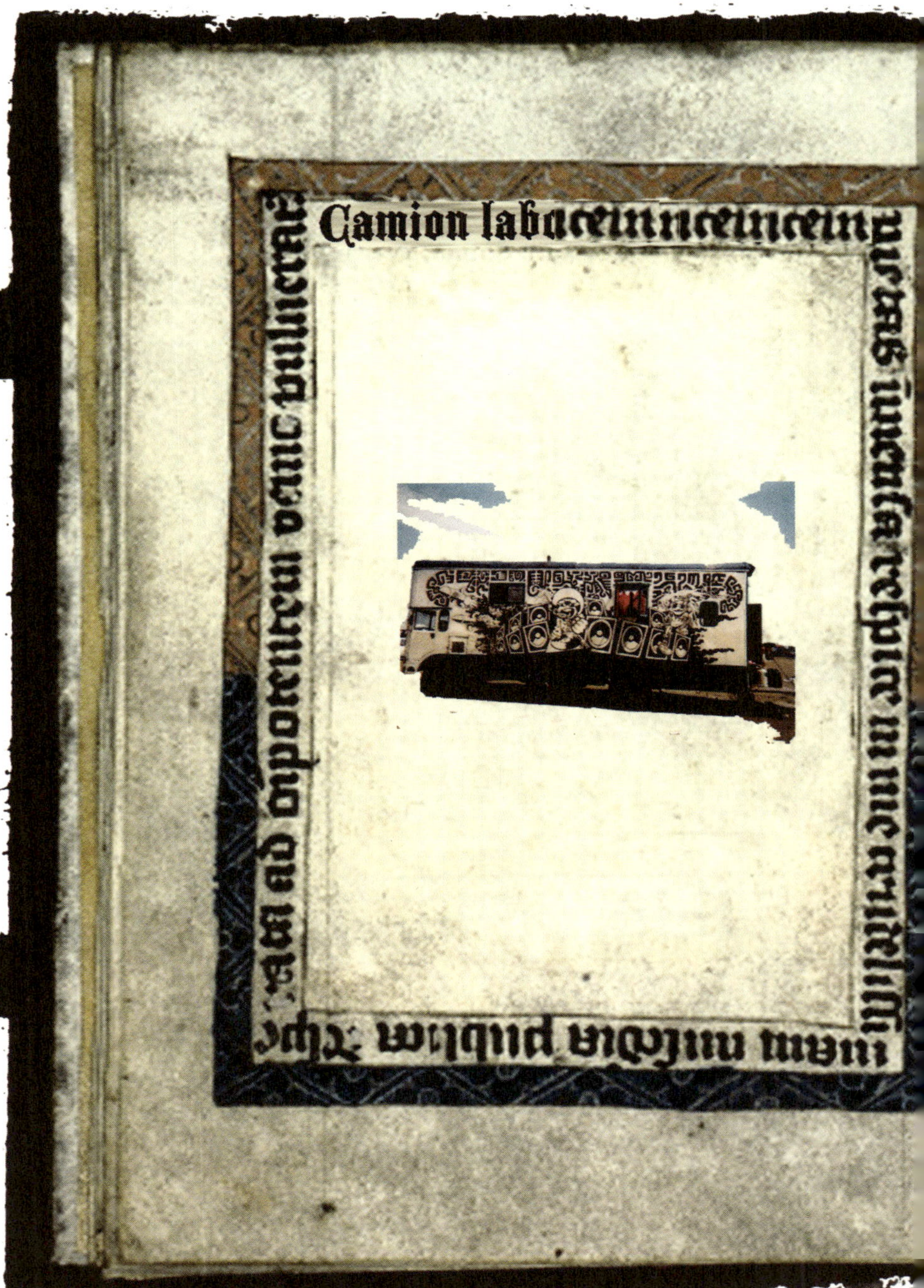
Camion laba

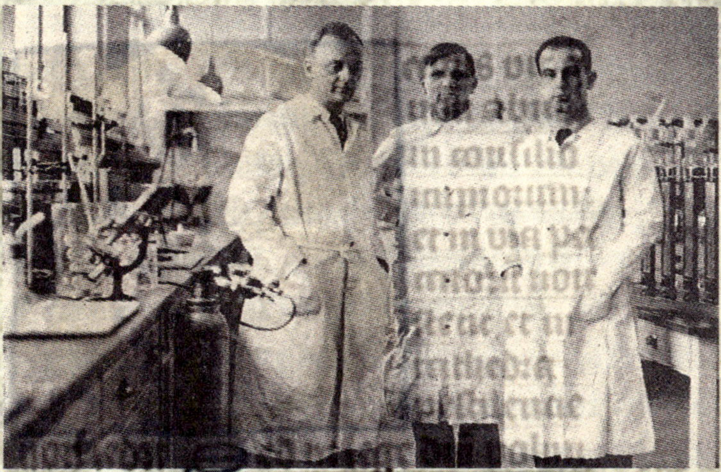

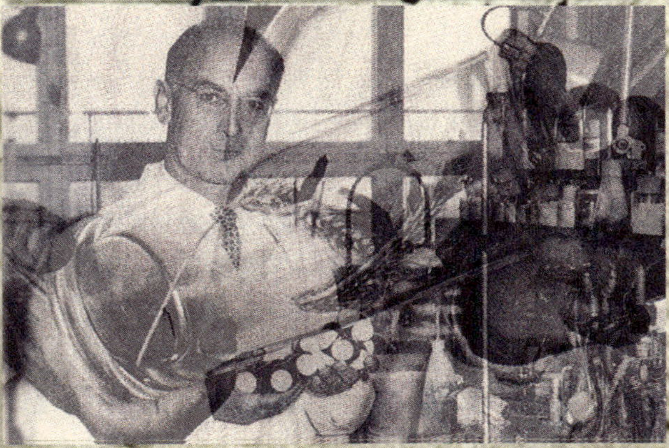

They had a drug: Unik.

Your drug doesn't have any effect on me.
It works with me, I don't get it.
Who gave you those phials?
The LSP, as usual.
You mean the stalkers. Those guys follow the convoys without speaking to anybody. How can you buy their pharmaceutical stuff, Matt?
To get to know what they are after.
But look, their VW is clean, as if they've just come out of the car-wash.
We could learn a bit more, since the occupants are at the sound system.
They've just pushed the door shut before marching off.

You see them?
No, they are at the sound system, I just told you. Give it to me, look, you turn this way, and then briefly that way, there you are.
Bloody hell, the cupboards are full of phials, all identical.
No, look there.
A smaller specimen.
Shall we taste it?
You first.

Matt? Answer me. Matt?

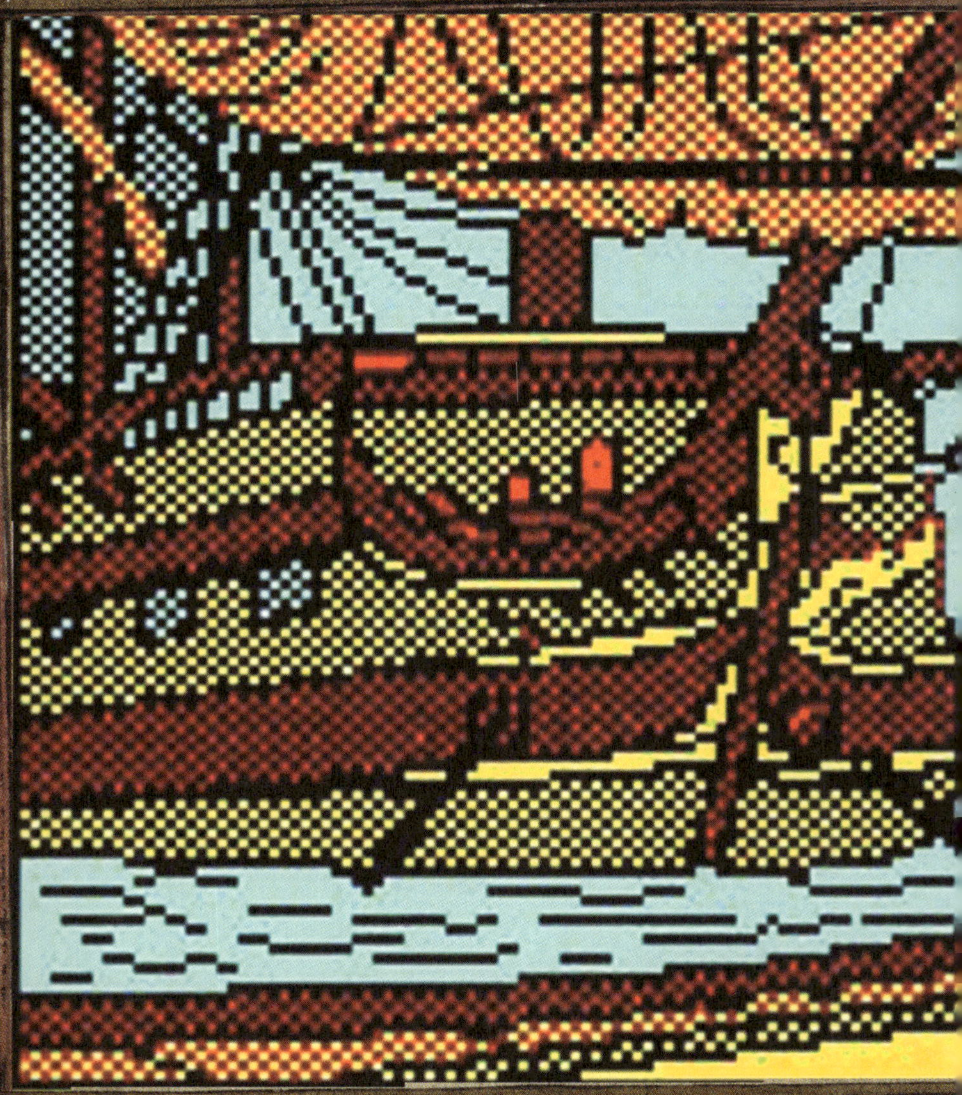

YOUR BOAT

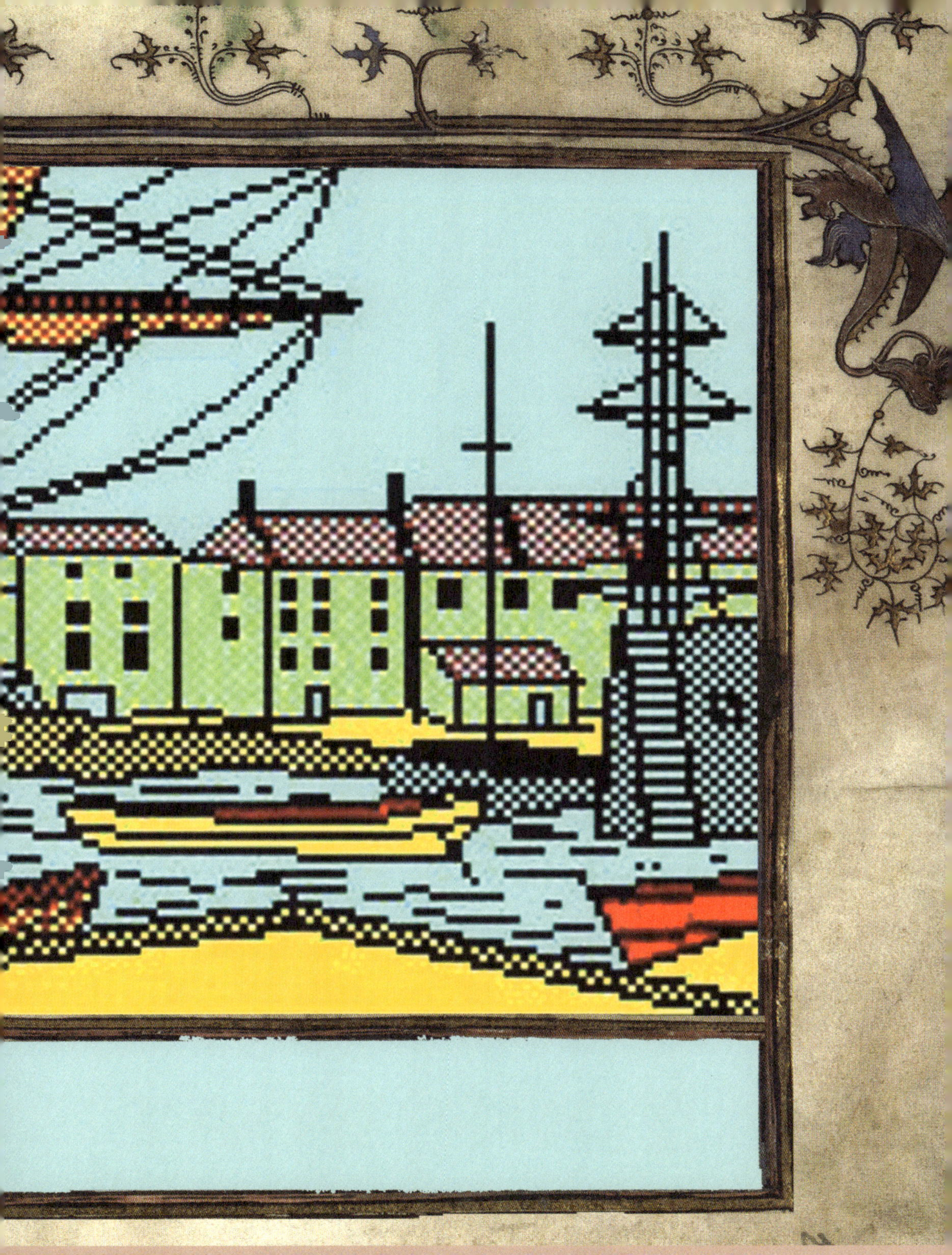

If Lenson doesn't have the reputation of a legendary pirate, it's because his project was different from that usually reserved for sea fighters greedy for riches, glory and victories. Lenson's fast frigate moved more quickly than any other ship of the time. Elusive, escaping early during battle, dealing with incomplete victories, the gang chief seemed to be willing to sneak along rather than board the commercial vessels in order to become self-sufficient.

His ship had been spotted in the North Atlantic, beneath the trade winds, even in Argentina according to some reporters. He would surely have been a good explorer for the East India Company, for his raids were plentiful, and one wonders at his capacity to keep going for such a distance without any supplies. What kind of crew follows someone like that, with no compensation other than rare calls at some islands? What crew can boast about firing cannons for a few minutes only before rushing into the wake of the belligerent, as if it was admitting defeat?

The historian, Ibarra Guzes, a specialist in anarchism, finds a seductive explanation there. Lenson's companions boarded at various places around the ocean. Some came from Bournemouth, others from Norfolk, North Carolina, still others from Cherbourg, and all of them had the plan to escape a certain form of civilization. Lenson successfully convinced them to settle in a virgin land somewhere in Argentina, to found a libertarian and sovereign colony. For that purpose, they needed a swift vessel; they had to race to attack ships loaded with supplies, then to make their way to a remote base acting as a new city. Those neo-sailors also had to toughen up for they were carried more by an ideal than by a taste for adventure. So his frigate was ploughing the ocean, avoiding encounters with any ship first, then going into occasional battle as soon as the crew appeared to have learned enough things. The most amazing thing is that this crew didn't hesitate to fight war vessels in the same way as they fought commercial ones. For about three years, Lenson was feared, but his loot was so insignificant that the naval powers didn't try to catch him. When, satisfied with his dearly acquired load, he withdrew to his new large-scale farming, there were few out there to complain, nor enough to build a solid reputation for him.

N OT DREAM

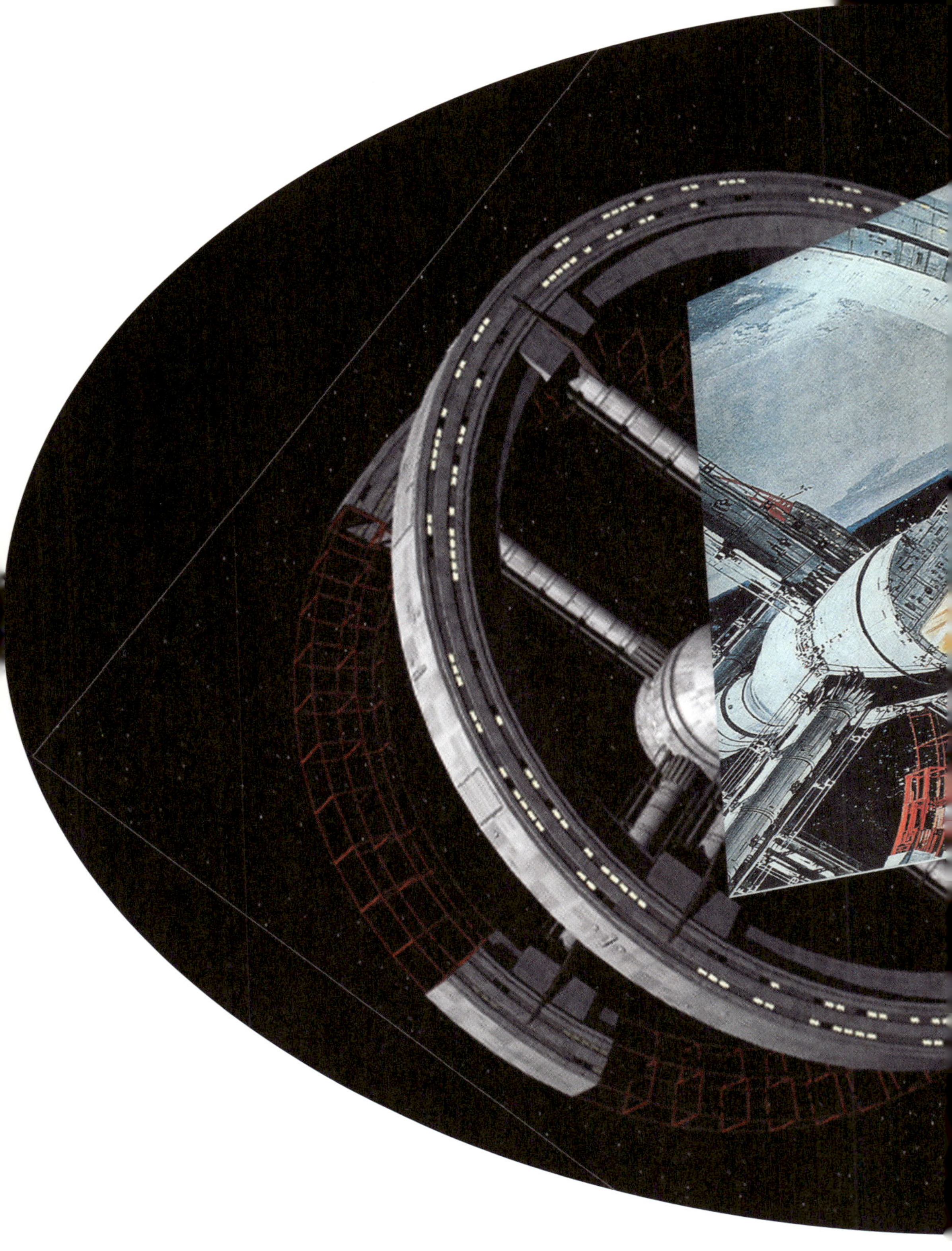

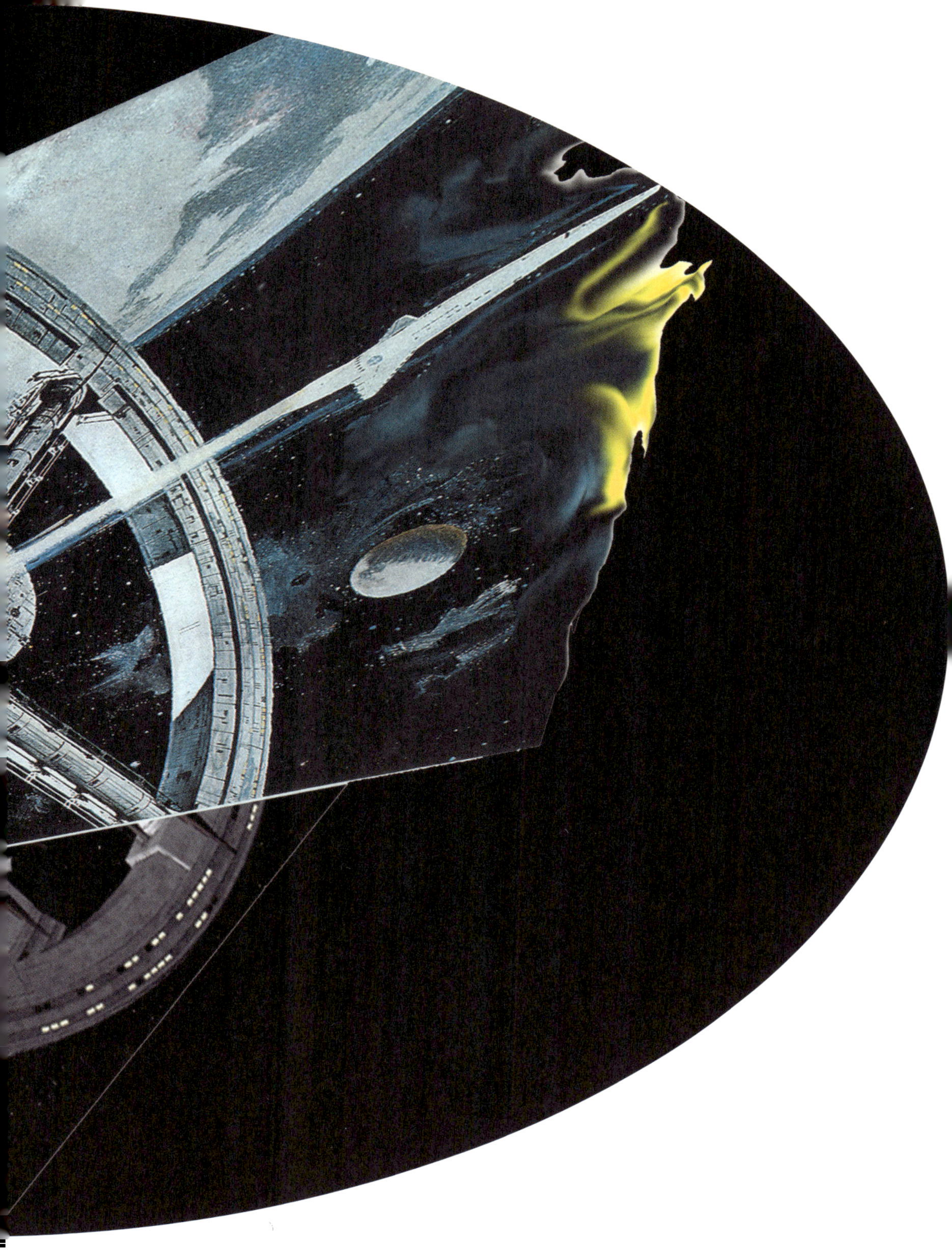

The *Cecilia* base is established on Martian land and sets out a quasi-total autonomy. Communications are rare: once a week with the ORBITA mothership responsible for selecting and redirecting the results of the work towards the countries taking part in the project. The base is organized according to a system devoid of hierarchy where each technician alone tests the compatibility of the material with the local environment and keeps a record of his own samples. He communicates his synthesis directly to ORBITA without reporting to the other technicians in order to avoid the results being selected by the fifteen member strong team. The internal organization is based on the free adherence to domestic tasks, on avoiding the formation of clans, on agreement and discussion for the missions putting together several colleagues, on the possibility even to renounce a mission if mutual understanding is incomplete. The scientific synthesis of the Cecilia micro-society is produced by ORBITA in relation to individual transmissions.

N O T DREAM

Matt? But where were you? We spent the whole morning looking for you.
I swallowed a drop of that stuff, then nothing.
What d'you mean, nothing?
I think I walked quite a bit.
Yes, we didn't say anything, you looked fine.
But I was fine. I marched to the beach. I saw a half-buried bunker. I went in it. I slept. I dreamed of a shadow shaped like a wolf. It made me laugh. I woke up with the feeling that a person dressed in a cape was guarding the entrance. There was a soft, oblique light. I came back. There, nothing.
Did the tide wake you up?
Why?
Your baggy is soaked.

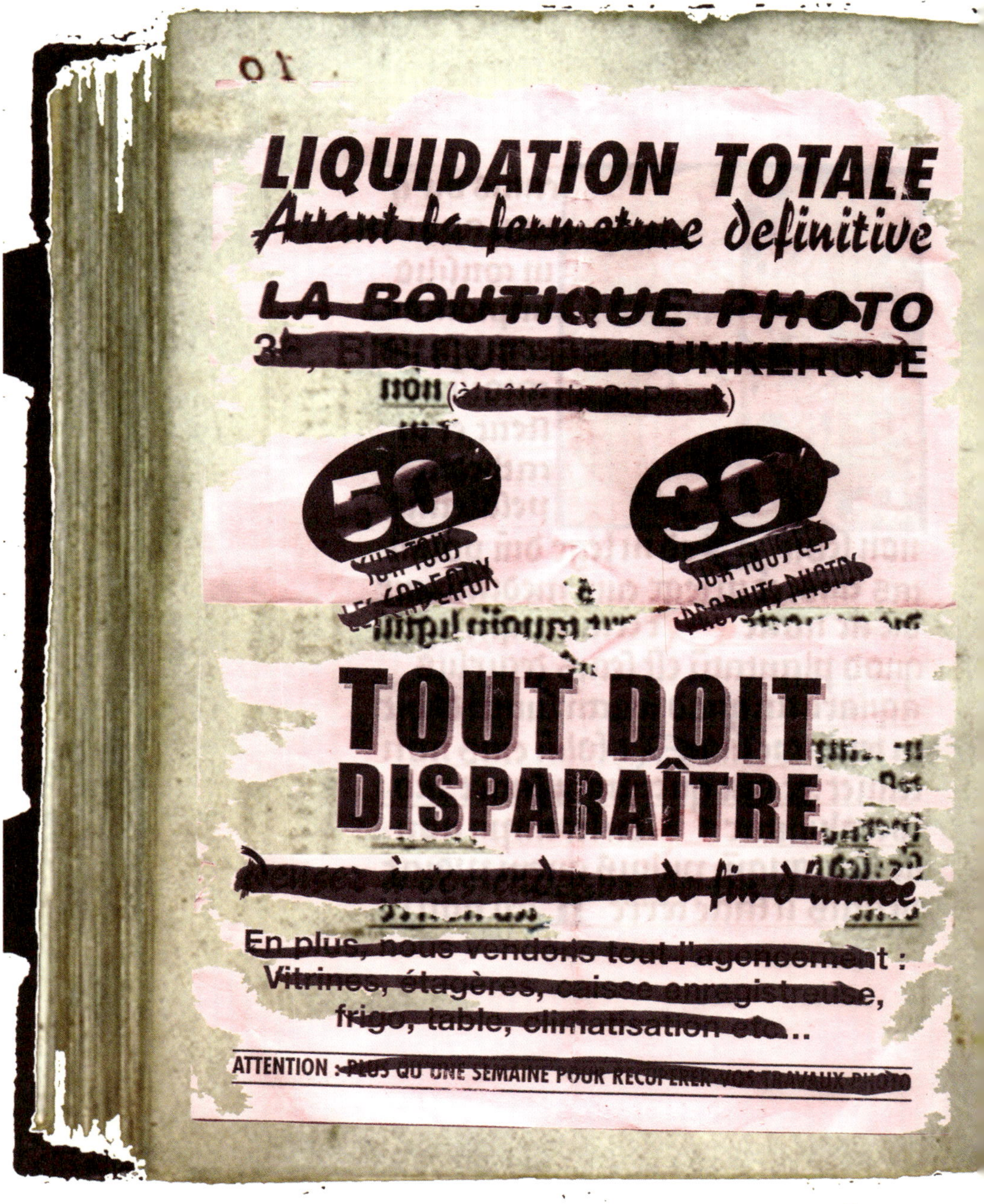
LIQUIDATION TOTALE
definitive
LA BOUTIQUE PHOTO
TOUT DOIT
DISPARAÎTRE
En plus, nous vendons tout l'agencement :
Vitrines, étagères, caisse enregistreuse,
frigo, table, climatisation etc..
ATTENTION :

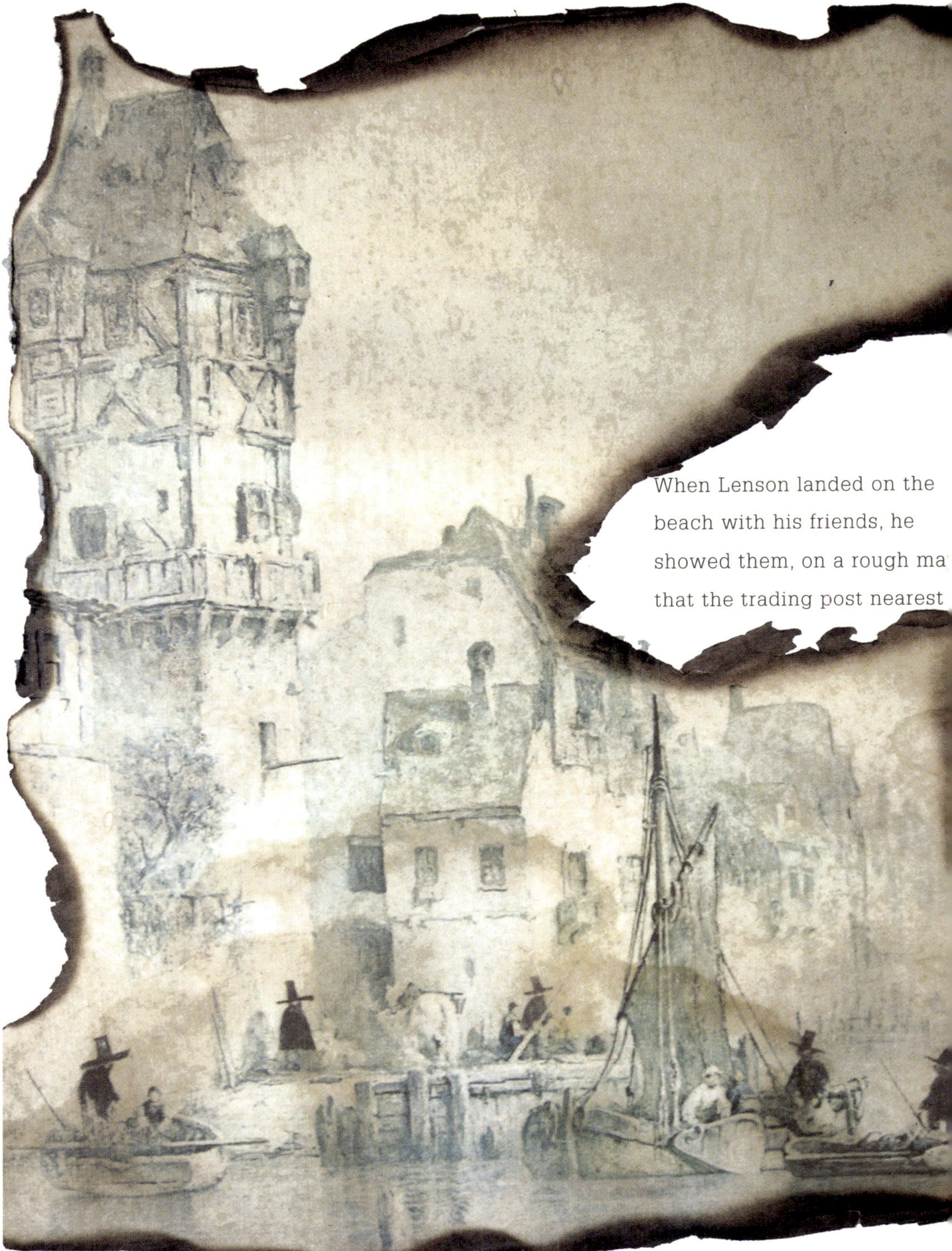

When Lenson landed on the
beach with his friends, he
showed them, on a rough ma
that the trading post nearest

heir new city was called *Cilia*.
At the suggestion of one of
hem, they adopted the name
Cecilia.

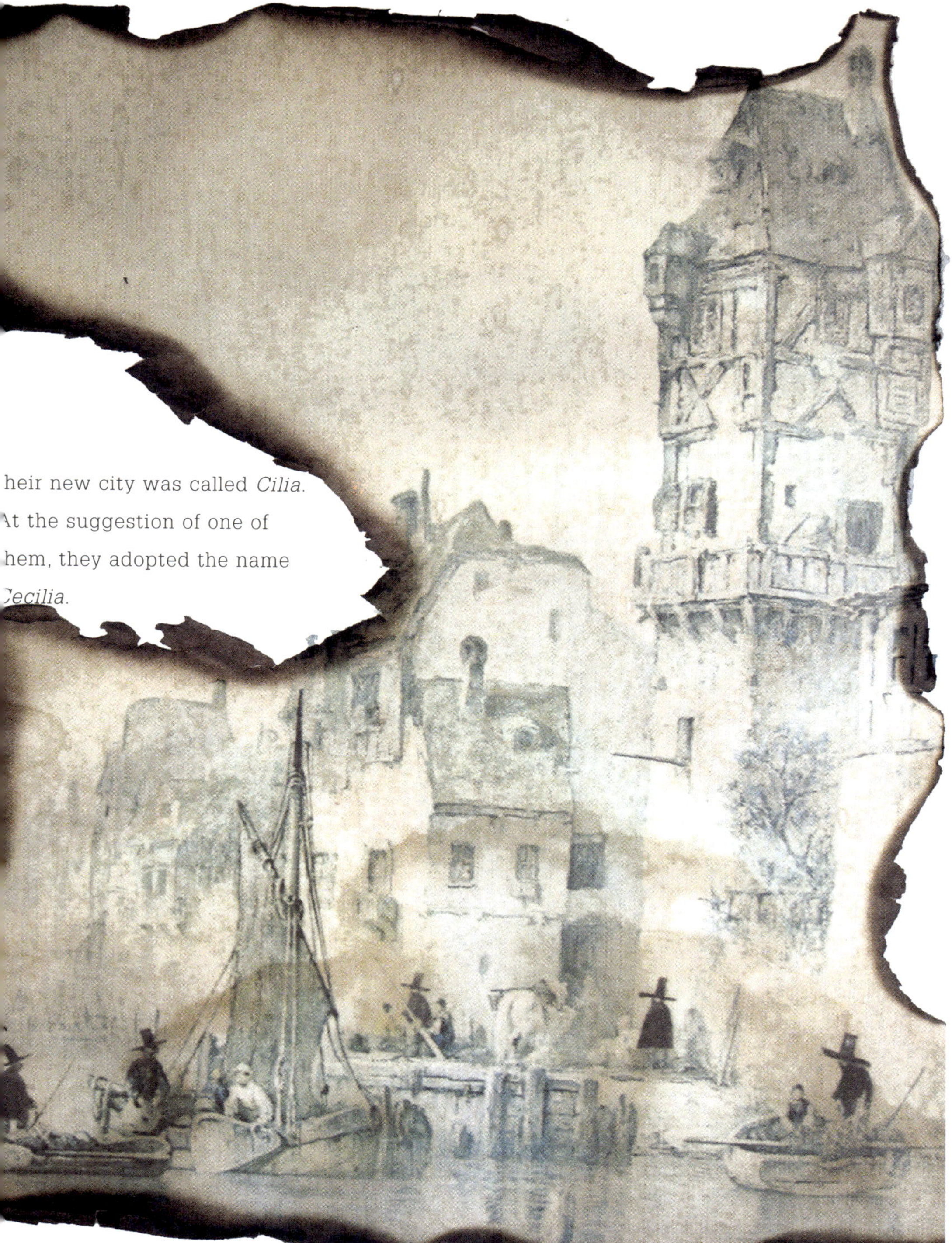

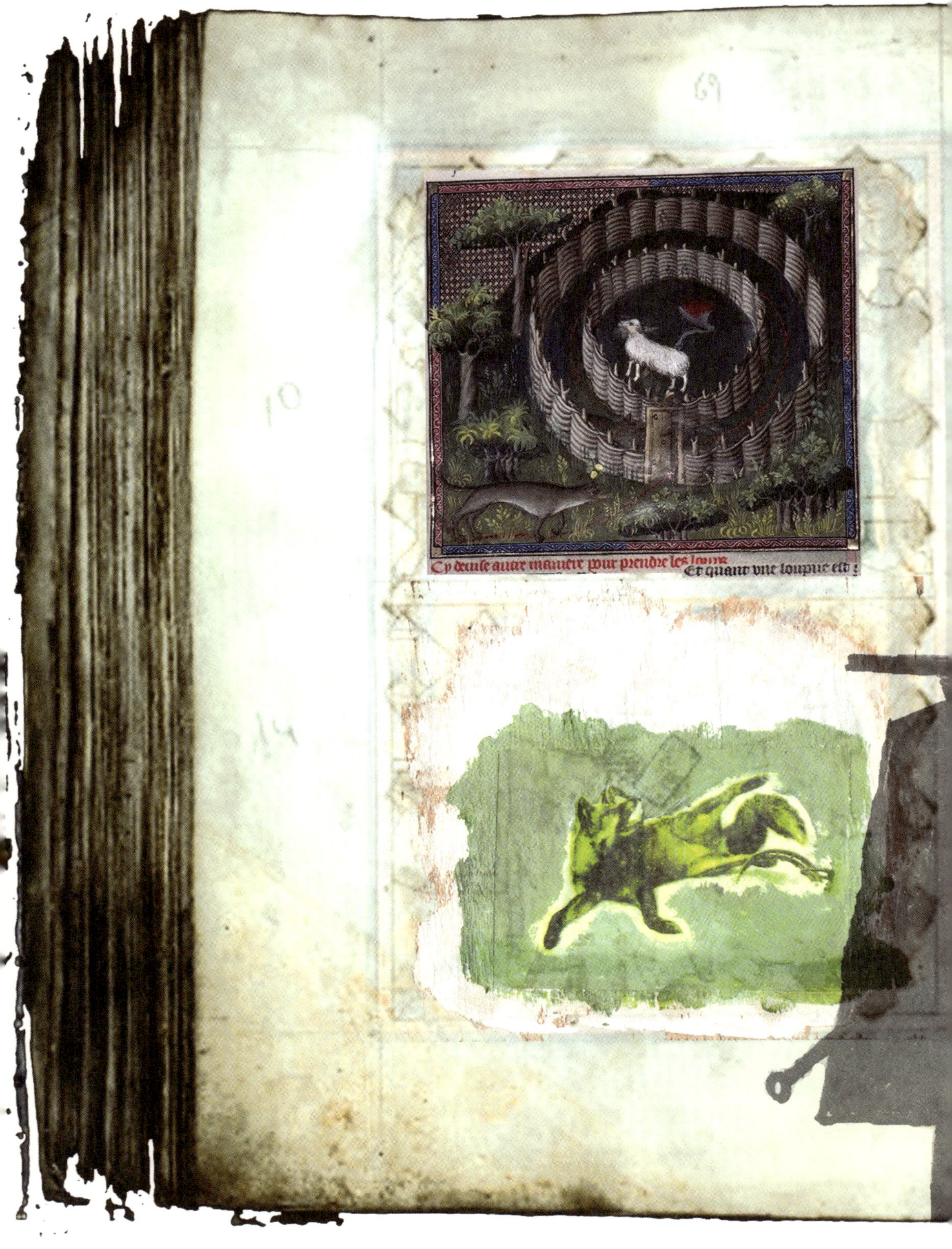
69
10
14
Cy deuise autre maniere pour prendre les loups
Et quant une loupue est

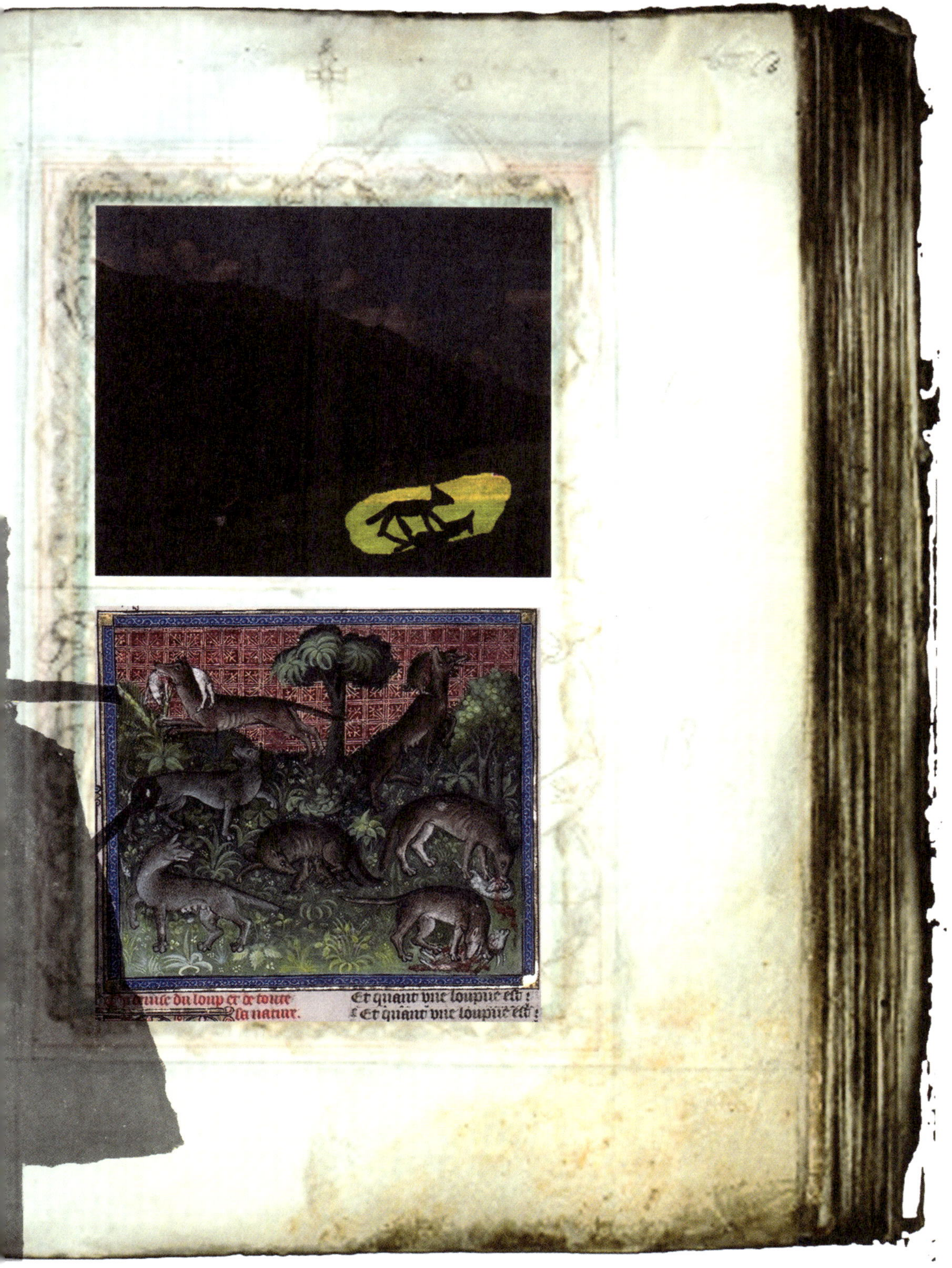
du loup et de toute
sa nature.
Et quant une loupue est
Et quant une loupue est

Matt, I've found something in a book about your wolf dream, look. The expert Mark H. Simmons talks about how he tried to analyze the remanence of the wolf in a patient's dream. It appeared in various roles and in various shapes related to everyday objects or popular expressions.

1. The wolf lives in a very hierarchical pack, structured by precise codes. The expert sees the connection between the patient and the collective and their shared actions.

2. The wolf's shadow, the haunting figure of the patient's dream, is the projection on the ground of the relation to the collective. Heavy or simply easier to control, the shadow is a two-dimensional reduction of a three-dimensional body, in other words: a restriction, but also a potential for the subordination of his desires. The collective becomes a sticky image, but one that can be observed from higher up with the pleasure one has in constantly redefining its contours.

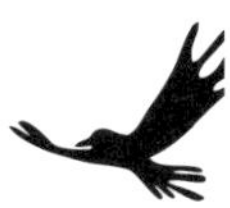

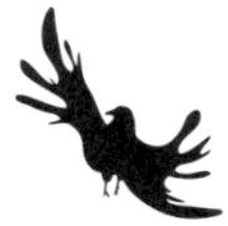

3. The wolf doesn't signify ambition, contrary to popular belief, but refers to the pack. To dream of a wolf means first of all that one will have to deal with a third person or with several individuals who will represent a potential for domination or subordination.
4. Simmons talks about the white wolf, usually meaning some kind of reputation, but here relating to a famous pirate feared for his tricks, whose notoriety was his white flag which appeared entirely white when seen from far away, but which revealed a lion's mouth when one came closer. What was first perceived as surrender turned out to be a cunning trap. His patient had dreamed of the shadow of a white wolf projected on the snow, indistinguishable for it was white on white, haunting.

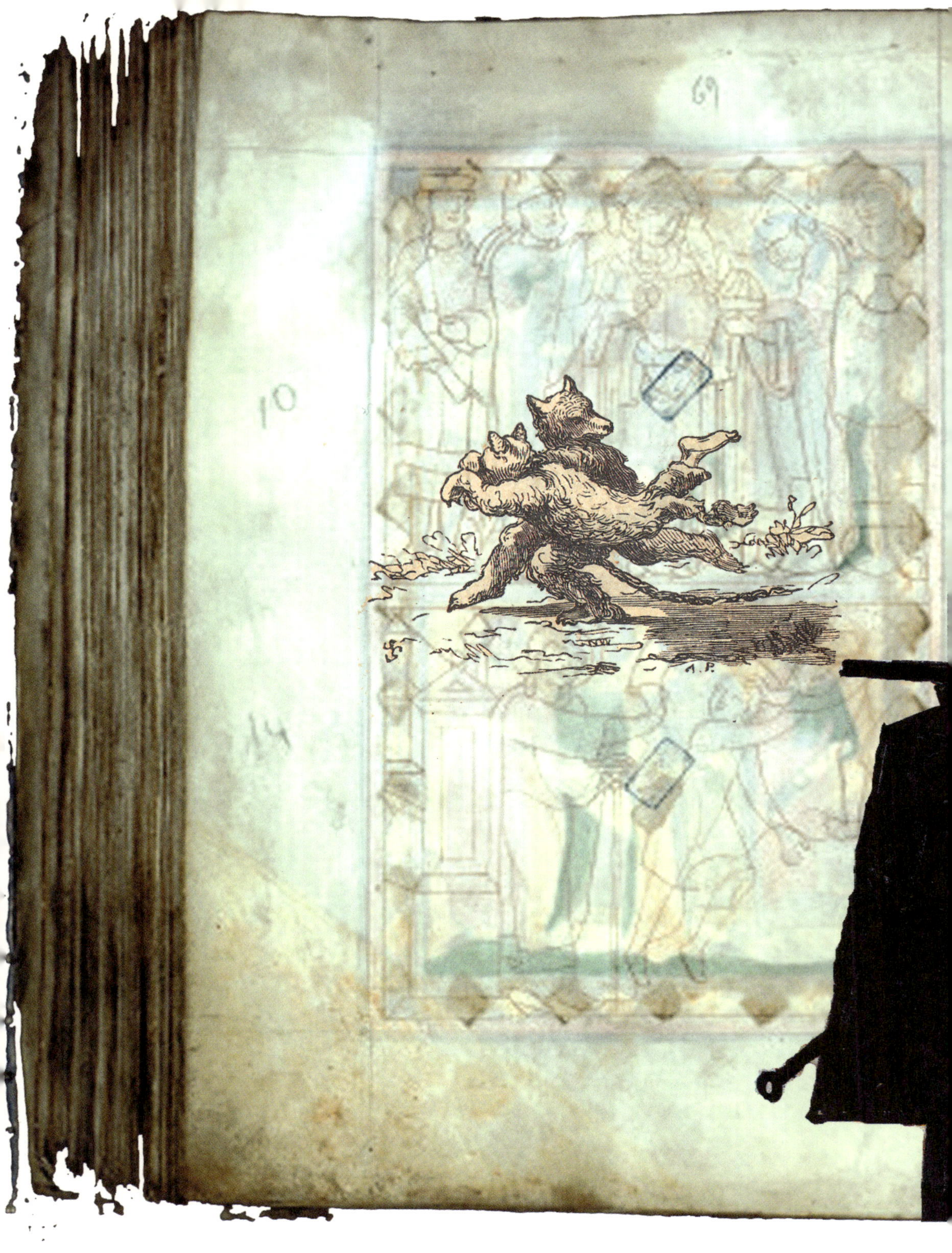
69
10
14
A.P.

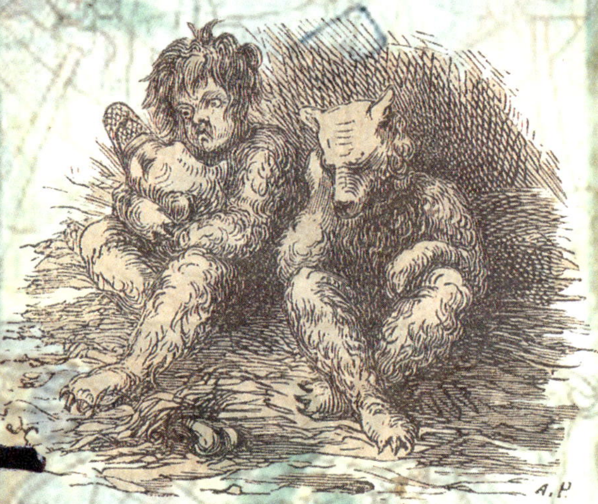
A.P.

He can hear a door opening; it's still dark. He's scared,
he's sweating. A door opens, he only sees legs.
He feels paralyzed.
His only thought. To leave.To escape.
He sees the outside between the legs and the door jamb.
He feels a blow. He yelps like a dog.
With an animal reflex he bowls into the man
Pushes the door open and flees.
He runs on a plain whose grass is green but it's like an animation.

All around is dark.
Below on the left there is a village.
The whole scene is lit by the moon.
It's a full moon. He looks before him,
then looks down and sees his shadow on the grass.
It's that of a wolf. He is a wolf.
He lifts his head and looks forward.
There is the edge of a forest. His only aim now
is to enter that forest.
He enters. It's calm. He walks, breathless.
Then he catches sight of another wolf on a rock
then another behind a tree.
Then another. It's a pack. He joins them, takes the lead into the forest.
Black.

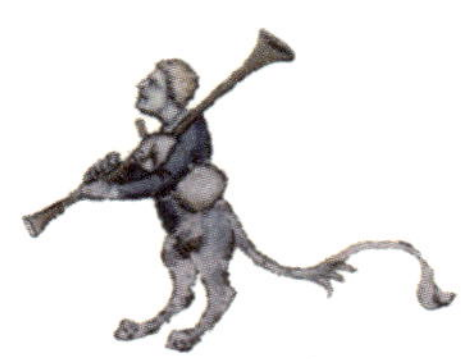

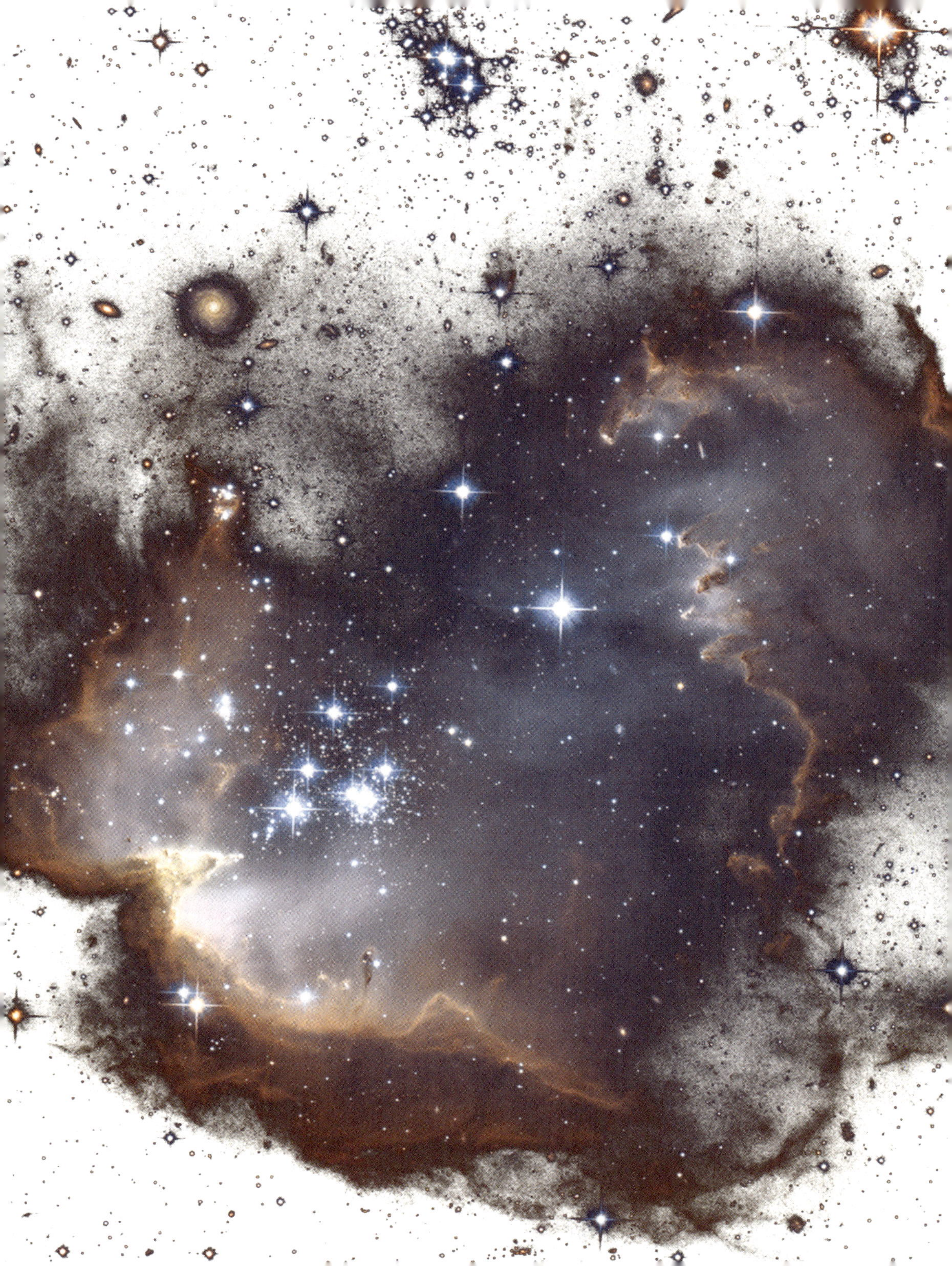

The event that happened on the Cecilia Martian base is of consequence as much for the history of space conquest and its unavoidable failures as for the history of the physical phenomena waiting still for a scientific explanation.
The 17 SP, the water tank of the main module, emptied totally into the equipment while the crew members were having a snack. The scientists were able to estimate the quantity of water provided for their needs when the level of flooding reached 75 cm over 110 m2. The main module is constructed of an assemblage of caissons, obviously waterproof, in order to maintain the atmosphere of the base, therefore, logically, the water, which had tools, sacks and clothes floating in it, could only stagnate. Panic took over the crew, their four companions who had remained outside, the ORBITA relay station as well as the operation centre.
Besides the risk of damaging the electronic material, the station was quickly turning into an impractical muddy site. The quantity of water to be evacuated was enormous, and each of the captives wondered how to proceed. But something as unbelievable as the incident itself happened: the water was drained in three minutes, as if a colleague outside had made water ducts 50cm in diameter with a drilling tool. No one could tell where the contents of the reserve had gone. They looked for a flow, a sheet of water, the porousness in the connecting elements: nothing. The relief was so great that it was only later that the question became of interest, particularly as the damages were numerous, and a program for reparations was needed first and foremost.

NOT DREAM

24 SP
Cecilia Base
KZ/LZ/MZ

New ground for tension, this time it concerns private property. Who can bring what without weighing down the transfer module whose weight has been carefully monitored? The book Li Roos has just found doesn't seem to have anything to do with the mission. Who hid it in her luggage? None of the sixteen scientists admit to it. Does one hide things or does one maintain a pretence of cohesion? It's okay not to be involved in others people's business, but the transfer module will bring back the whole crew to ORBITA once the mission is completed, so one may as well cooperate without shame and explain what a comic is doing in the main module.

NOT D REAM

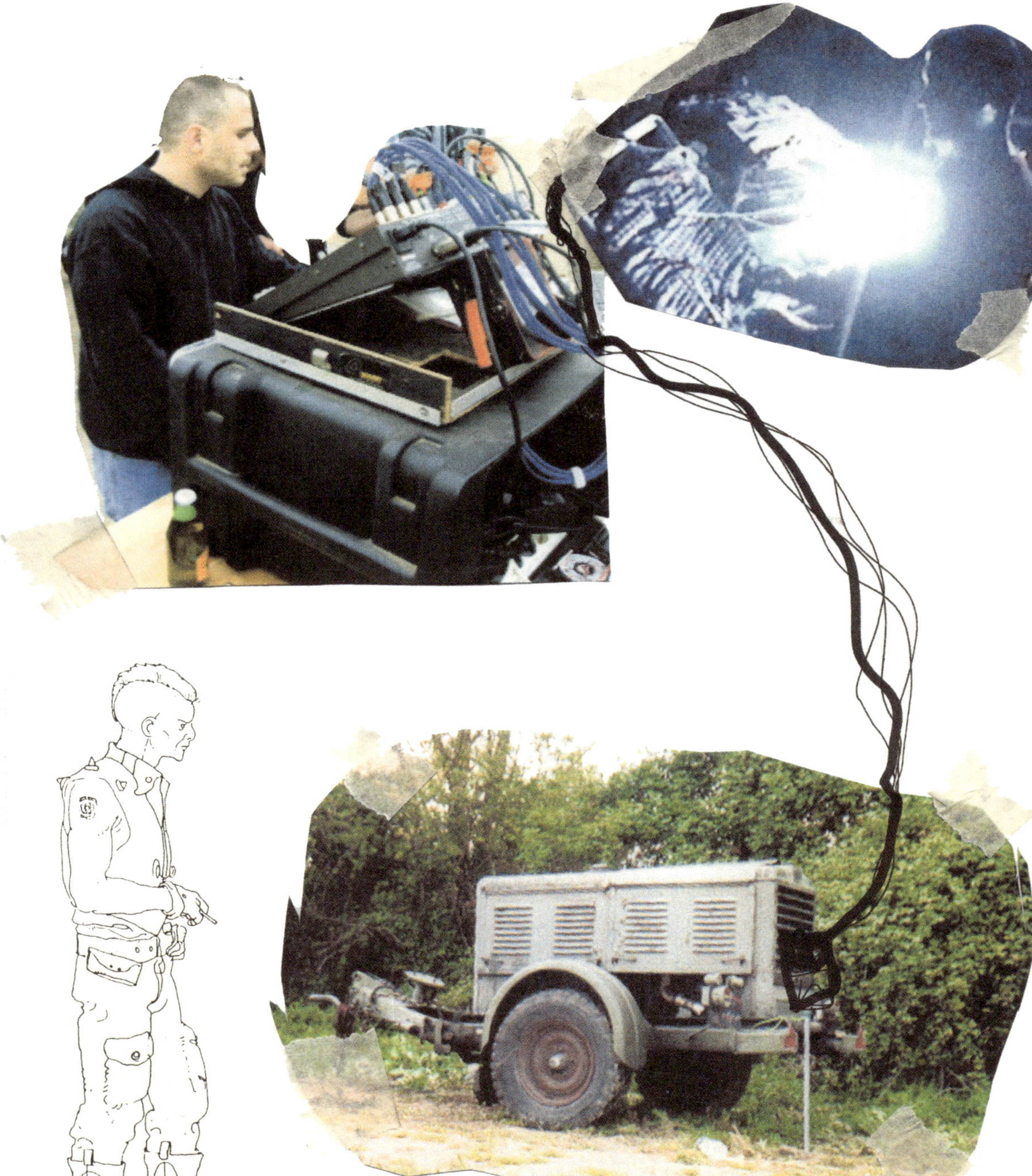

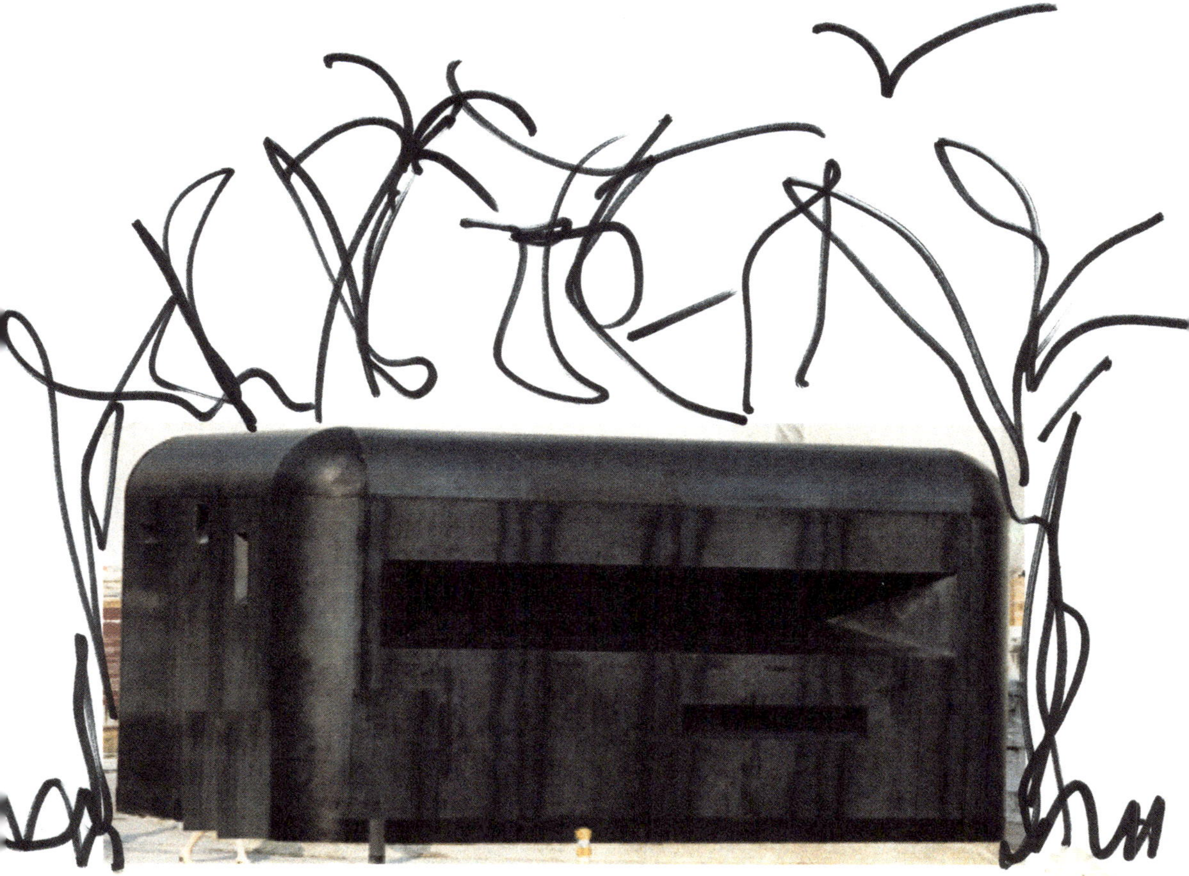

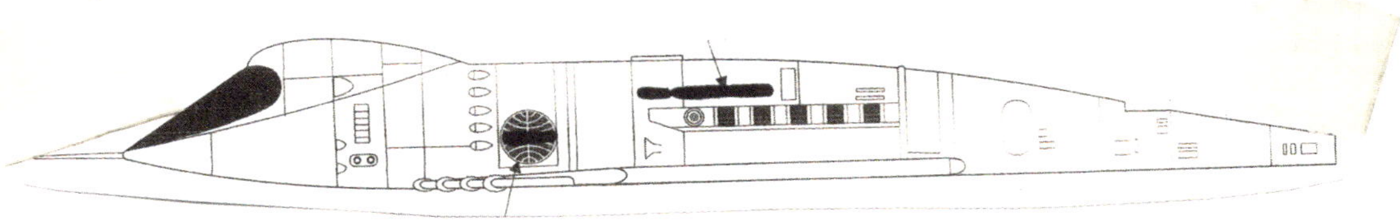

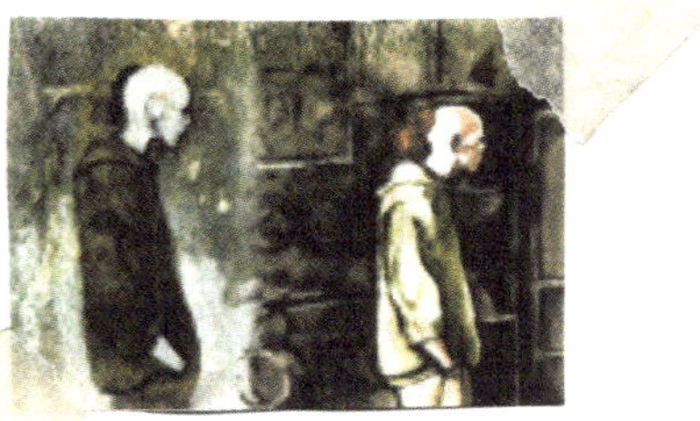

His first vision

If there is one person who remains sceptical of the whole Lenson project, it's White Wolf, the formidable pirate practising the open course to excess and eager to see, in his imitators, preys even more attractive. No, that principle of minute spoils leading to an Argentinian peaceful haven doesn't add up. According to White Wolf, that Lenson has invented a little legend in order to hide his hoard better and to devise a golden retreat in a forgotten place where no one would look for him. To find Lenson and his band of landlubbers becomes a priority. The white flag enters the bay of Cilia after five weeks hunting. The sardine boats of the Argentinian trading post are amazed to see a new three-mast ship settling in their sector, far from the channels. If they haven't had the curiosity to go and see what the other newcomers in their colony had been up to, now was their opportunity. Having reached the place, the locals just had the time to see Lenson's companions grab their boats and row in the direction of their frigate under the occasional gunshots fired from the beach. Rowing energetically, Lenson hears White Wolf belching, his feet deep in the water: look, that son of a bitch has left the hoard on board!

NOT DR EAM

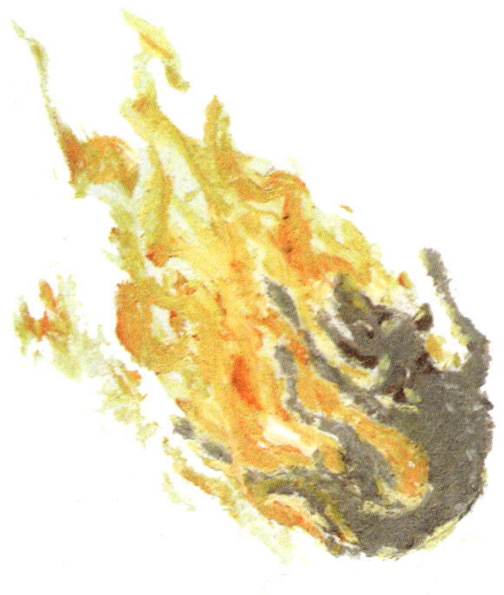

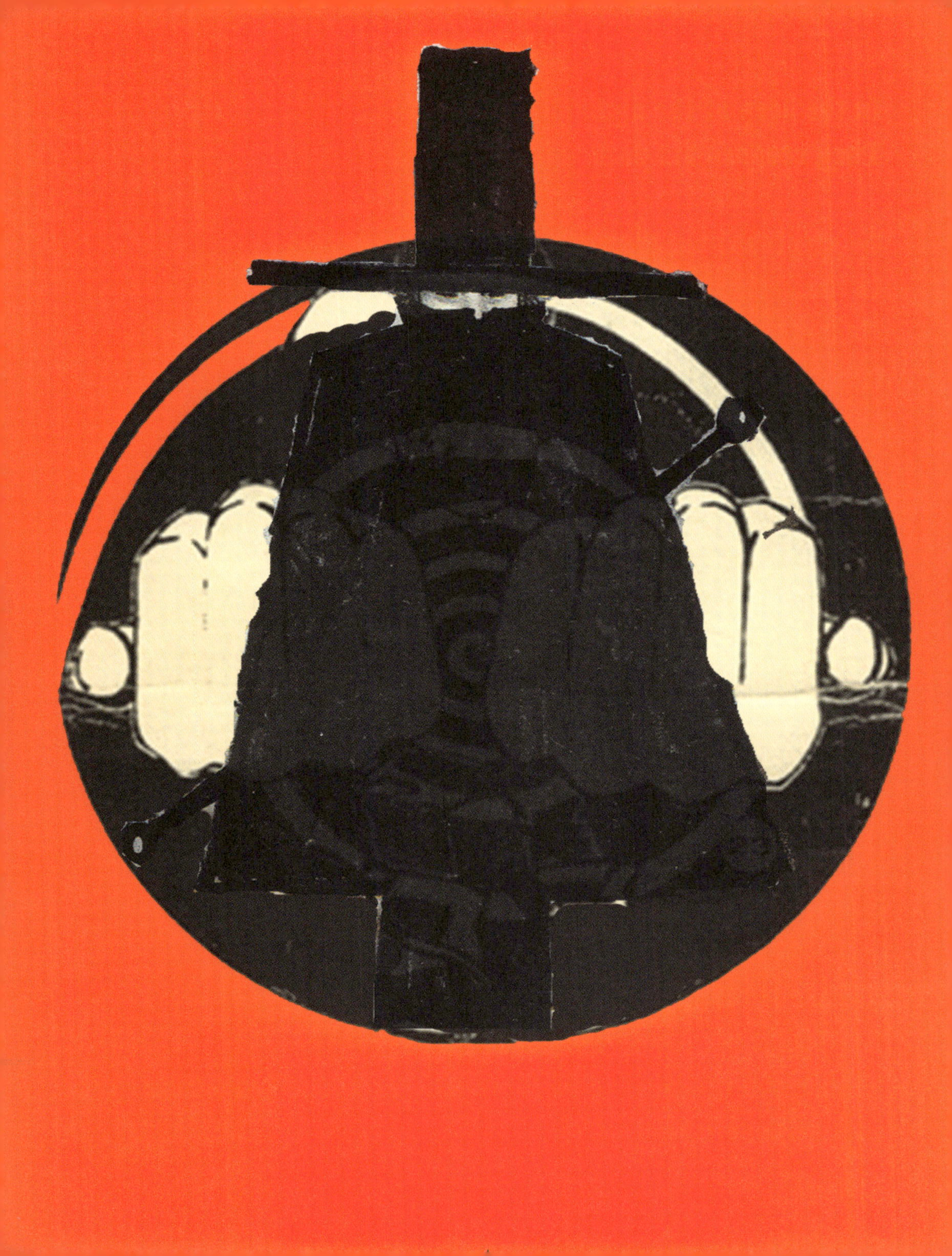

In the deep of the night
They crossed his path

He stretched out his hand
In the hollow, that end of road
Unïk
Quickly swallowed quickly carried away

The wolf shows the way
Through the wheel
Between earth and moon

Reality, the world of origin, far behind
Having arrived in a world of synthesis.

With the tip of his cane he draws a triangle on the ground,
Inside, a sphere, outside, another,
At their cosmic meeting
He is no longer.

We are looking for you Psychodrhomme, through time
YOU hold the key to the space
Which will allow us to be there and far at the same time.
In a beloved Ubiquity.

Look: I give you six matches, and you have to make four triangles.
What's that about?
I'm asking you to look for the answer.
Well, six matches, four triangles.

I I I I I I

No, I can't do it. Why that test?
The character wearing the cape traced six lines with his stick, then lifted them as if there was a magnet on the tip of each.
Is that the answer?
Yes, lift them to build a three-dimensional shape.
Did that character say anything else?
Yes, that what I've just seen was a footbridge.
Where is that bunker?
Let's go there.

Is that it?
Yes, that's the bunker.
It looks new.
That's where I slept.
Wait, there's a guy sleeping.
What's that shit? You have a twin brother, Matt?
What?
Look, he's your living image.
I don't understand.
You should, right?
No, let's go back.
Why? You can talk to us, we're your friends, no need to tell us that story of triangles.
Let's go back, for God's sake!

Steering South to circumvent the trade winds, then to the East towards the Cape of Good Hope and Madagascar. Lenson's ship is moored off an island overlooked by an imposing mountain. The place appears deserted and it's time for a rest and more so for there's a shaded cove to hide his frigate. The first night on the island is quiet. The camp is only temporary for the island resources prove to be insufficient to found a free colony there: some fruits, trees, a few insects, no game and a mountain so jutting that it's of no practical use. Lenson finds it hard to sleep, tormented by his speculations about the future of his small society: to go back to Argentina, to Cecilia, yes, but when? What if White Wolf returns there to wait for him? How to resume piracy in the South Atlantic when commercial vessels are so rare?
He finally falls into a gentle sleep.
Lenson is a sailor on a steamer + he receives his first corporal punishment at the hands of a wine waiter armed with a whip + devours a pineapple, eating only the flower, with some disgust + follows geese flying with his eyes when he is called in a foreign language + he's on the mountainous island and it's the chief of the Liber tribe who addresses him + his warriors are dressed in baggy clothes that blend with the surrounding greenery + they drag a cart loaded with extremely noisy chests + the chief of the Liber introduces himself: Psychodrhomme the First, historical king of the Liber + gathered around a drink kept in a triangular container, the king and his guest listen to the tales of the royal songster: how the chief of the tribe has become traveling wind + they propelled their canoes with a good haul favored by coastal winds

+ when a ship with no sail slowly approached their fishing nets + one could read its name in golden letters, on the hind: Psychodrome + it was steering at a right angle to compose a geometrical figure hard to distinguish from the canoes + after that it sailed away + the chief of the canoes felt strong enough to take up the name of the vessel + furthermore, that name would give him the strength to travel anywhere he saw fit + Psychodrhomme the First could therefore pay a visit to New Amsterdam's quays, replenish Drake, sail in the midst of the Armada, untie Ulysses from his mast, supply provisions to the Mayflower and stroke White Wolf.

Lenson starts involuntary, jumps out of his bed, scrutinizes the horizon; the night is quiet, his companions are sleeping peacefully, the sentry is joyfully drumming with his fingers on the pole where he remains on duty. Lenson falls back to sleep.

A week goes by before that same sentry suddenly becomes agitated: White Wolf! Look, there! The white flag signaling the headstrong pirate is hoisted up. But who could have informed him of the frigate's improvised stopover? Lenson himself didn't know that he would find that island which hadn't been marked on the marine map yet. Chance, surely, and the opportunity for White Wolf to also have a rest after the exhausting chase.

DREA M

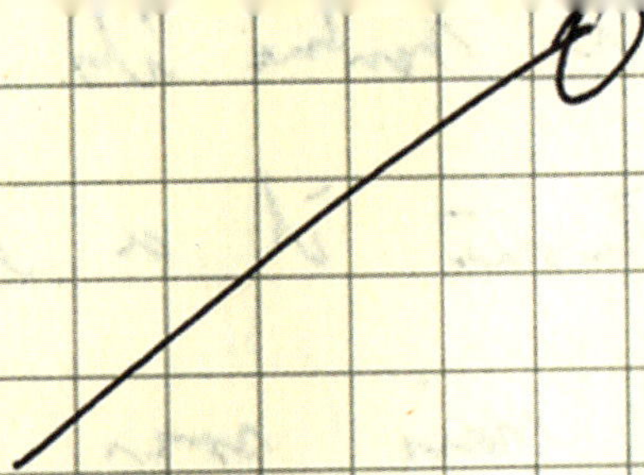

1' 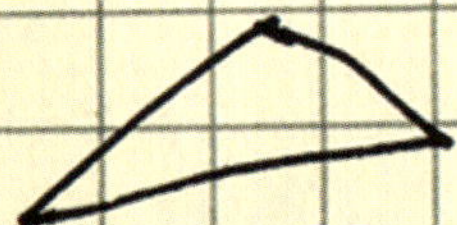

2' 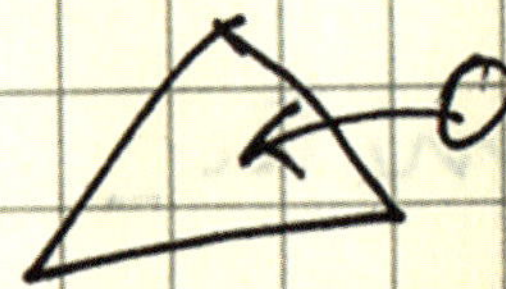

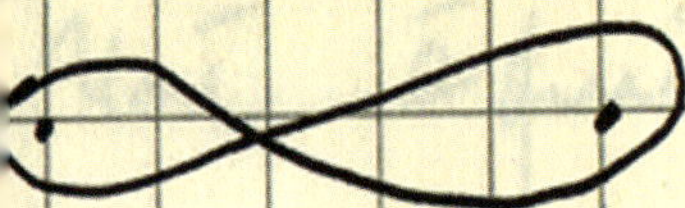 le Temps

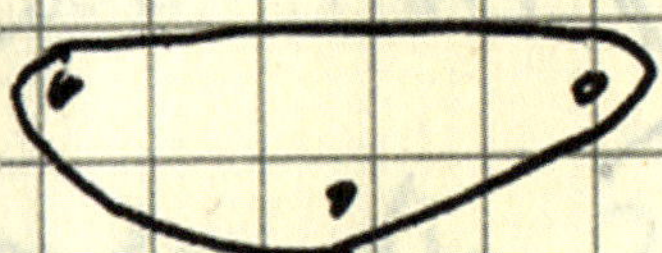 l'espace

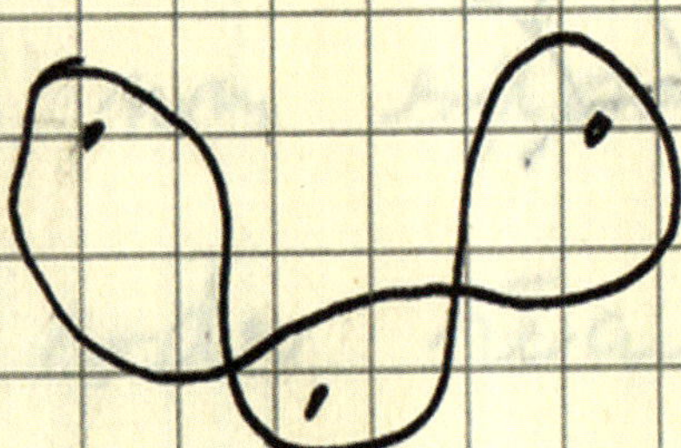

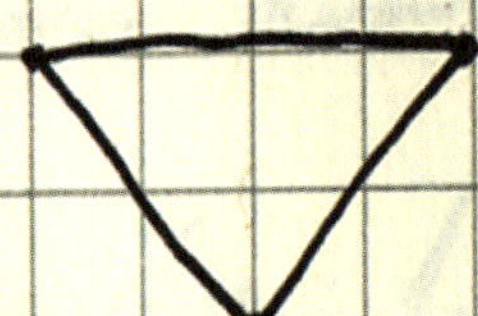

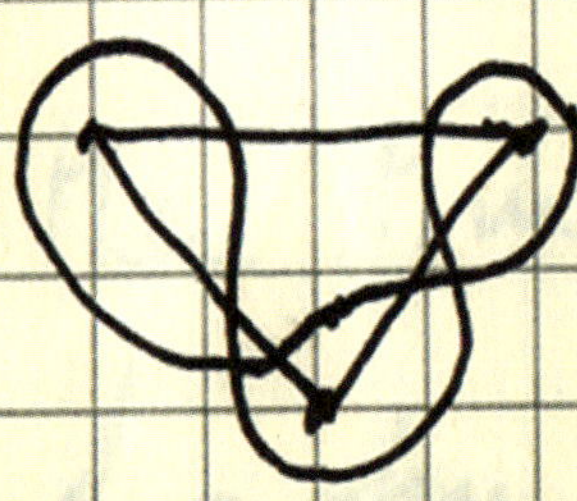

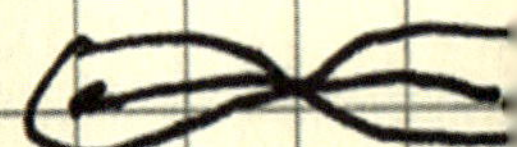

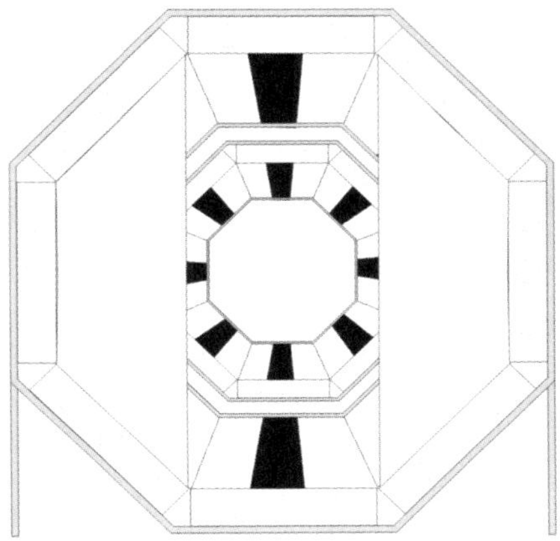

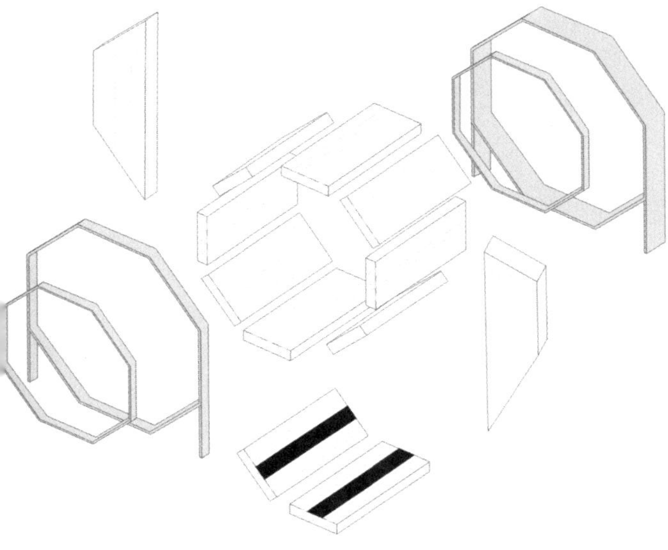

They initiate him in the crossing

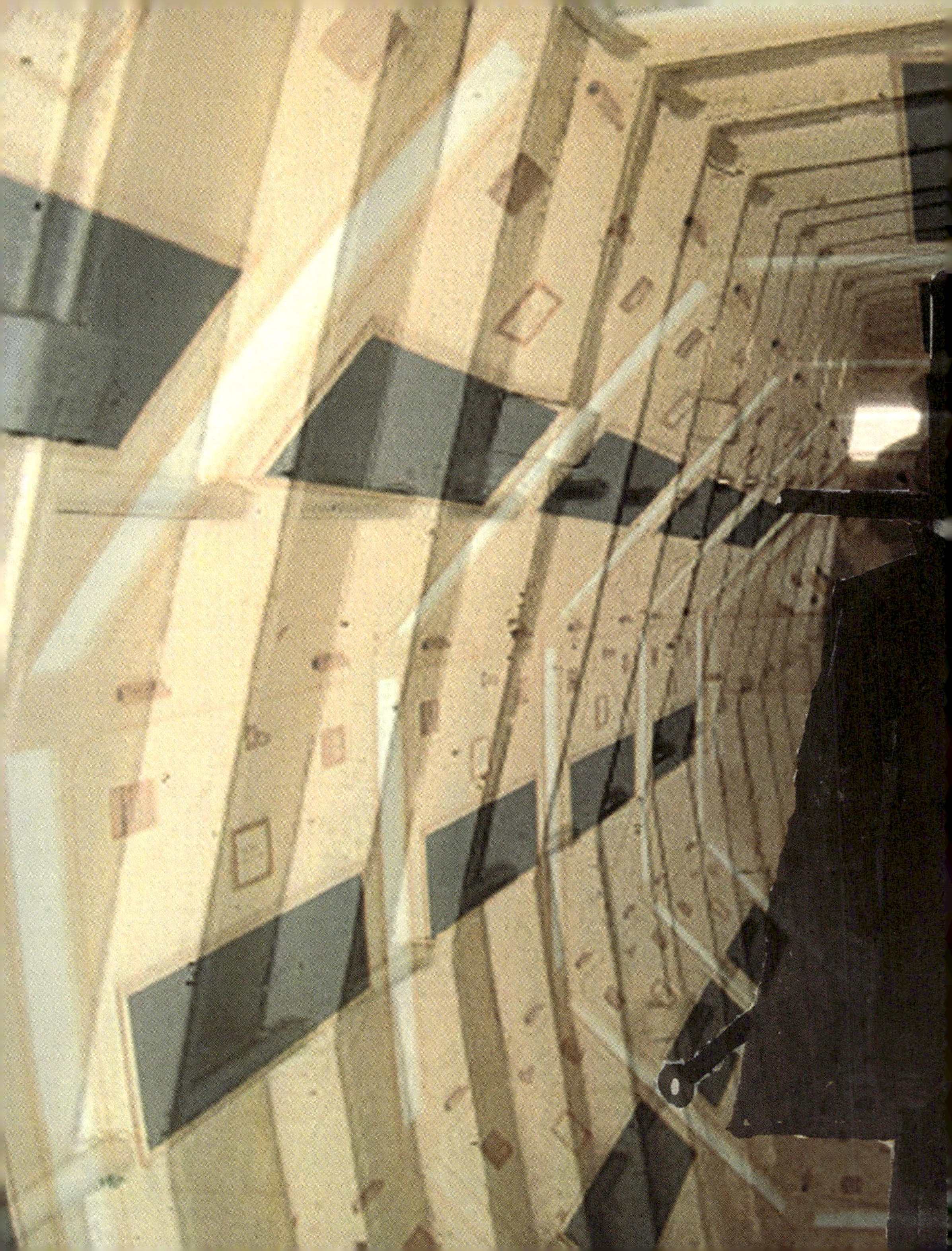

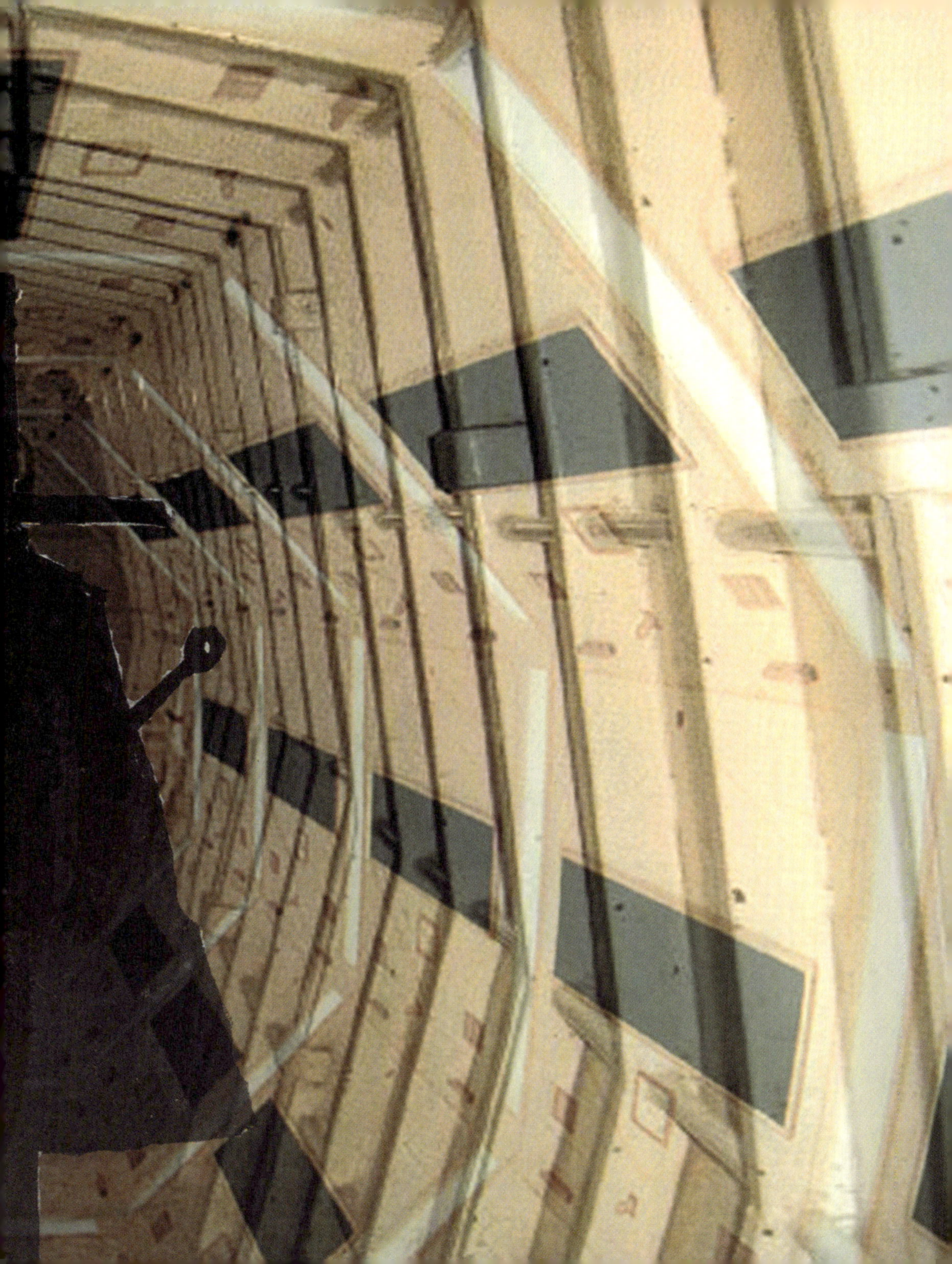

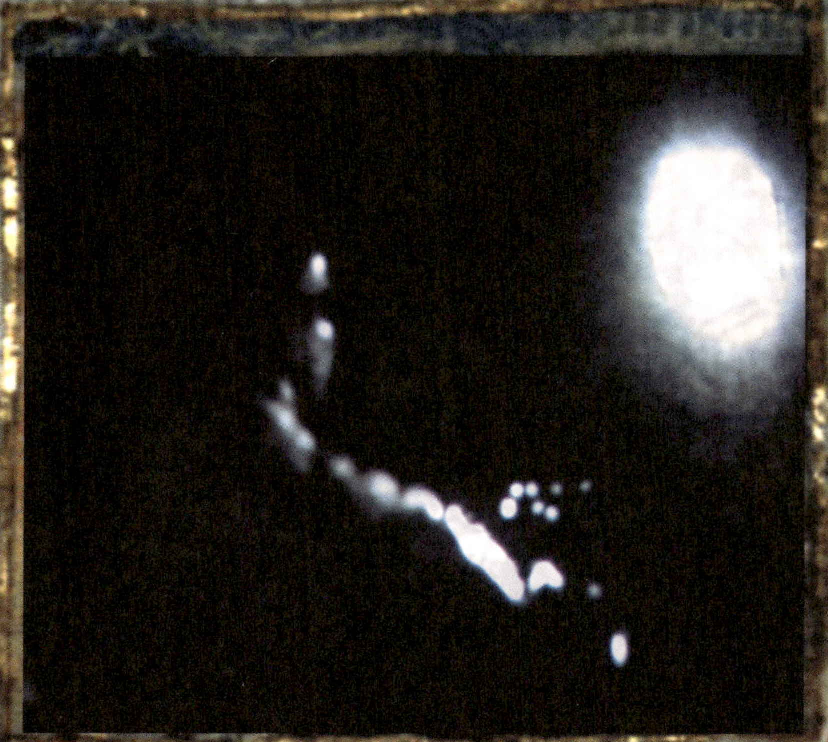

To find it again we become two. We are not one person in two places but one person in each place.

Matt, you must go back there.
You go back to the bunker.
You want to know who's that look alike.
When you are on the bunker's threshold, you can see him sleeping.
He wakes up, gets up without seeing you, leaves the bunker, direction: the party.
You follow him.
He trips on a root, just as you did.
He goes back to his mates' VW and explains what he did after he took some of the phial's contents.
You hear him say: But I'm fine. I marched to the beach. I saw a half-buried bunker. I went in. I slept. I dreamed of a shadow shaped like a wolf.
You don't even dare to intervene.
Anyway, your friends only talk to that new Matt.
They don't actually see you.

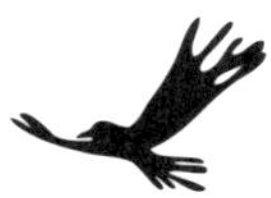

FEBRUARY 1975

A LIGHT VESSEL FROM THE INDONESIAN NAVY INTERCEPTS A BOAT THAT HAS JUST ENTERED ITS TERRITORIAL WATERS. THE TOTAL LACK OF SIGNALING FROM THE SHIP INDICATES IT'S A DRIFTING STRUCTURE. THREE SAILORS AND AN OFFICER STEP FOOT ON THE DECK AND BEGIN AN INSPECTION. THE OFFICER INFORMS HIS SUPERIOR OF THE SHIP'S EXCELLENT CONDITION WITH THE EXCEPTION OF THE MISSING MASTS, A FACT IMPOSSIBLE TO EXPLAIN. THE COMMANDANT REPLIED THAT SOME AUSTRALIANS HAVE RECENTLY SHOT A CLOAK-AND-DAGGER FILM OFF THEIR COAST. HE SEES THAT SHIP AS A REPLICA OF A VESSEL CONSTRUCTED FOR THE FILM, THEN LEFT ABANDONED. ONE OF THE SAILORS VENTURES INTO THE DEEPEST HOLD AND SHOUTS: CAREFUL, IT'S SINKING, IT'S A METER DEEP, AND IT'S GETTING HIGHER! THE OTHER SAILORS AND THE OFFICER RUSH IN TO SEE, FIND THEIR COMPANIONS STAGGERED, POINTING AT WHAT THE FOUR OF THEM TESTIFIED TO HAVING SEEN: THE HOLD EMPTYING ITSELF IN A FEW MINUTES. THAT DUBIOUS TESTIMONY HAS SOMEHOW WEIGHED HEAVILY ON THE MILITARY CAREER OF THE FOUR INDONESIANS WHO MAINTAINED THE SHIP HAD EFFECTIVELY DRAINED ALL BY ITSELF.

DREAM

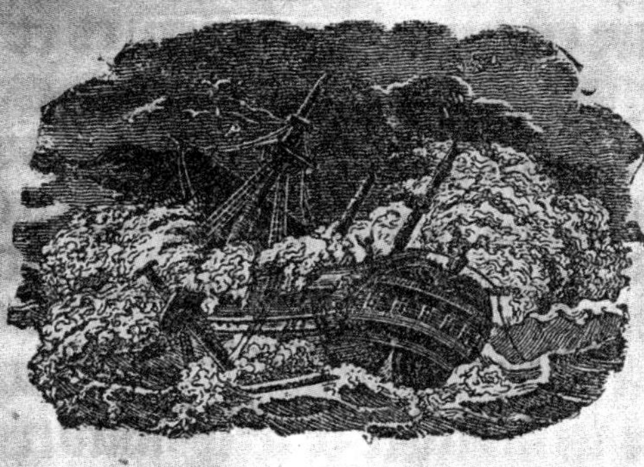

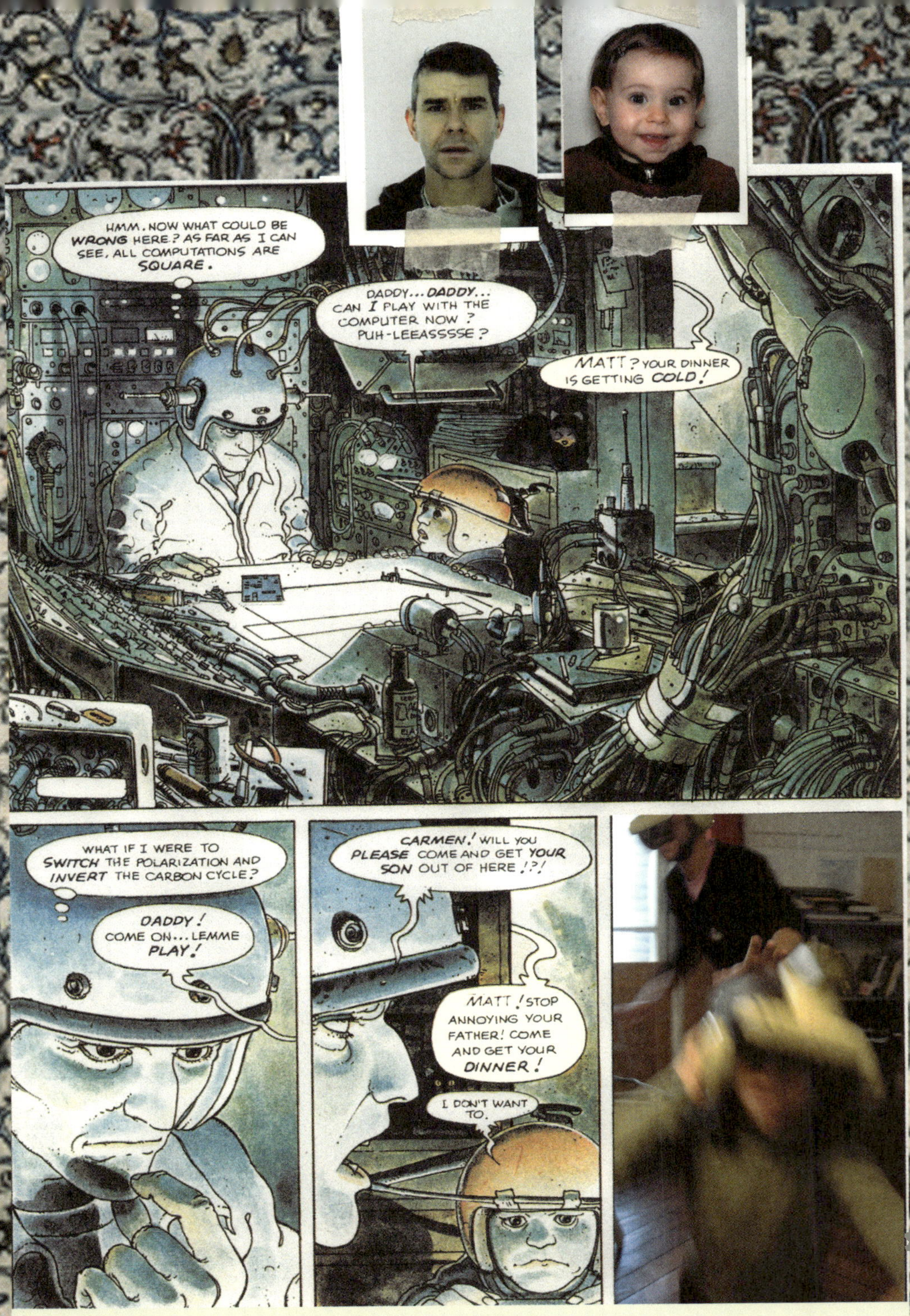

But sometimes men from the original space try to penetrate the space of synthesis.

You go back to the bunker.
You see yourself in front of the entrance, your friends at your side.
One of them shouts: what's that shit, you have a twin brother, Matt?
You looked embarrassed, then you advise them to go back.
You stay behind.
You look at that pseudo-twin who sleeps next to a strange boiler suit.
He wakes up, slips into it.
His crash helmet shows that he's going to enter an oxygen-free zone.
The bunker is filling with water.
The flood reaches your knees before you get scared and run away to the campsite.
Breathless, in a state of complete panic, you need to talk to your friends and find the clearing where the free party unravels.
The vehicles are just lining up.
There, you see yourself at the wheel, parking your VW, chatting with a girl friend.

WHEN THE CRETAN PHILOSOPHER EPIMENIDES DECLARED HE WAS A LIAR, HE WAS ILLUSTRATING ONE OF THE PROBLEMS IN LOGICS DEBATED FOR SO LONG IN ANTIQUITY BY NUMEROUS PHILOSOPHY SCHOOLS. YES, FOR IF HE IS REALLY A LIAR, HE'S LYING, THEREFORE HE IS NOT A LIAR. THOSE IMPASSES OF LOGICS, AS THEY ARE CALLED, IMPRESSED THE MATHEMATICIAN KURT GÖDEL AT THE TIME HE WAS TACKLING THE QUESTION OF WHETHER ANY MATHEMATICAL THEORY COULD LEAD TO A CONTRADICTION. HIS WORK SHOWS THAT IN ARITHMETIC PROPOSITIONS EXIST ABOUT WHICH IT'S IMPOSSIBLE TO DECIDE IF THEY ARE INFALLIBLE OR NOT. TODAY, THE INFALLIBILITY OF A PROPOSITION IS PART OF THE OPTIONS FOR ANSWERS TO ANY MATHEMATICAL QUESTION.

ONCE YOUR VW IS PARKED, YOU OFFER SOME PHIALS TO YOUR FRIENDS WHO SEEM PUZZLED.

YOU TELL THEM WHERE YOU GOT YOUR SUPPLIES.

THEY DISAPPROVE.

THE VAN YOU ARE POINTING TO IS A VEHICLE FOR MEDICAL EMERGENCIES.

THE PEOPLE OCCUPYING IT ARE DRESSED IN WHITE BLOUSES.

LOCKING THEIR VAN, THEY JOIN THE FIRST TECHNO CIRCLES AND THEIR DANCERS.

YOU FORCE THE LOCK.

YOU AND YOUR FRIENDS RANSACK THE SHELVES UNTIL A PHIAL DRAWS YOUR ATTENTION.

YOU GRAB IT, BREAK A TIP THEN THE OTHER TO ALLOW THE CONTENTS TO FLOW.

BUT THE LIQUID REMAINS CONGEALED IN ITS GLASS PHIAL.

YOU SHAKE IT, WONDERING ABOUT YOUR FRIEND, WHO ALSO GIVES IT A TRY.

YOU TAKE IT FROM HIS HAND AND NOW YOU HAVE THE FEELING THAT THE GLASS IS MELTING.

THE PHIAL BECOMES AS LIQUID AS ITS CONTENT.

THERE, YOU HURRY DRINKING IT, IN ONE GULP.

YOU SLOWLY LEAVE THE VAN BENEATH YOUR FRIEND'S EYES LOOKING FOR YOUR FIRST SENSATIONS.

YOU PENETRATE DEEP INTO THE FOREST THAT BORDERS THE CLEARING.

COMMUNICATION FROM THE OPERATION CENTRE TO THE PRESS

THE CECILIA PROJECT CARRIED OUT ON ONE OF OUR MARTIAN BASES IN THE SECTOR AUX VENTS, PRODUCES AN ENTIRELY ORIGINAL VISION OF SCIENTIFIC EXPLORATION.

1. FIRST THE NAME: CECILIA, GIVEN NOT WITH THE PURPOSE OF AN EAR-CATCHING SWEET SLOGAN, BUT IN REFERENCE TO THE ATTEMPT BY GIOVANNI ROSSI TO SETTLE A LIBERTARIAN COLONY ON A TERRITORY FREE FROM ANYONE'S CLAIM. THAT ITALIAN ANARCHIST HAD CONVINCED HIS COMPANIONS TO FOUND A LONG-LASTING SETTLEMENT IN BRAZIL WHICH WOULD SERVE AS AN EXAMPLE FOR THE NASCENT 19TH CENTURY ANARCHIST MOVEMENT.

2. THEN THE CONCEPT: TO SET TO WORK 15 SCIENTIFIC ENTITIES THAT WOULD BE FREE, INDEPENDENT, UNCONTROLLABLE, SOVEREIGN, AND SEE IF A SYNTHESIS OF THEIR SOLITARY WORKS COULD PROVE MORE EFFICIENT THAN THOSE CARRIED OUT BY OBEDIENT, UNITED TEAMS.

3. ANTICIPATED RESULT: TO FEED THE RESEARCH OF THE THINK TANK KZ/LZ/MZ AROUND A REFLECTION ON CYBERNETICS/COMMUNITY/CONFLICT/SYNTHESIS.

OUR FIRST LESSONS ARE THAT THE IMPORTANCE OF THE MISSION AND THE SERIOUSNESS WHICH SURROUNDS IT ARE SUFFICIENT TO VALIDATE A FEELING OF REALITY FOR SCIENTISTS WHO ARE HOWEVER THE OBJECTS OF PURE SIMULATION. THEIR RELATIVE ISOLATION AND THEIR PRIDE PROBABLY FORBID

THEM TO QUESTION THE REAL NATURE OF THEIR MISSION. NEEDLESS TO SAY THE OPERATION CENTRE ALONE IS AWARE OF WHY THE CECILIA PROJECT IS SO SPECIFIC. THEY HAVE NO IDEA OF THEIR THWARTED AND CLOSELY OBSERVED FREEDOM. THEY THINK THEIR DIFFERENT NATIONALITIES EXPLAIN THE PARTITIONING OF THE TASKS.

EVEN THE MOST EXTRAVAGANT SITUATIONS, THOSE WE HAVE IMAGINED, HAVE RELATIVELY LITTLE INCIDENCE ON THEIR PERFORMANCE. PANIC HAS UNITED THEM, THE RETURN TO NORMALITY HAS ISOLATED THEM AGAIN, THE IMPONDERABLE HAS EVER SO SLIGHTLY MOVED THEM. THEIR REACTIONS HAVE SHOWN ONE COULD ADAPT TO THE INCONGRUOUS AS WELL AS TO REALITY, AS LONG AS THE SCIENTIFIC MISSION PREVAILS.

A QUESTION REMAINS THOUGH: WHO HAD THE IDEA OF PLACING A SUPERNUMERARY BOOK IN THEIR BELONGINGS? WHY DID THAT BOOK APPEAR AFTER OUR CONJURER'S FLOOD? IN SHORT, WHO TOOK THAT INITIATIVE AT OUR EXPENSE?

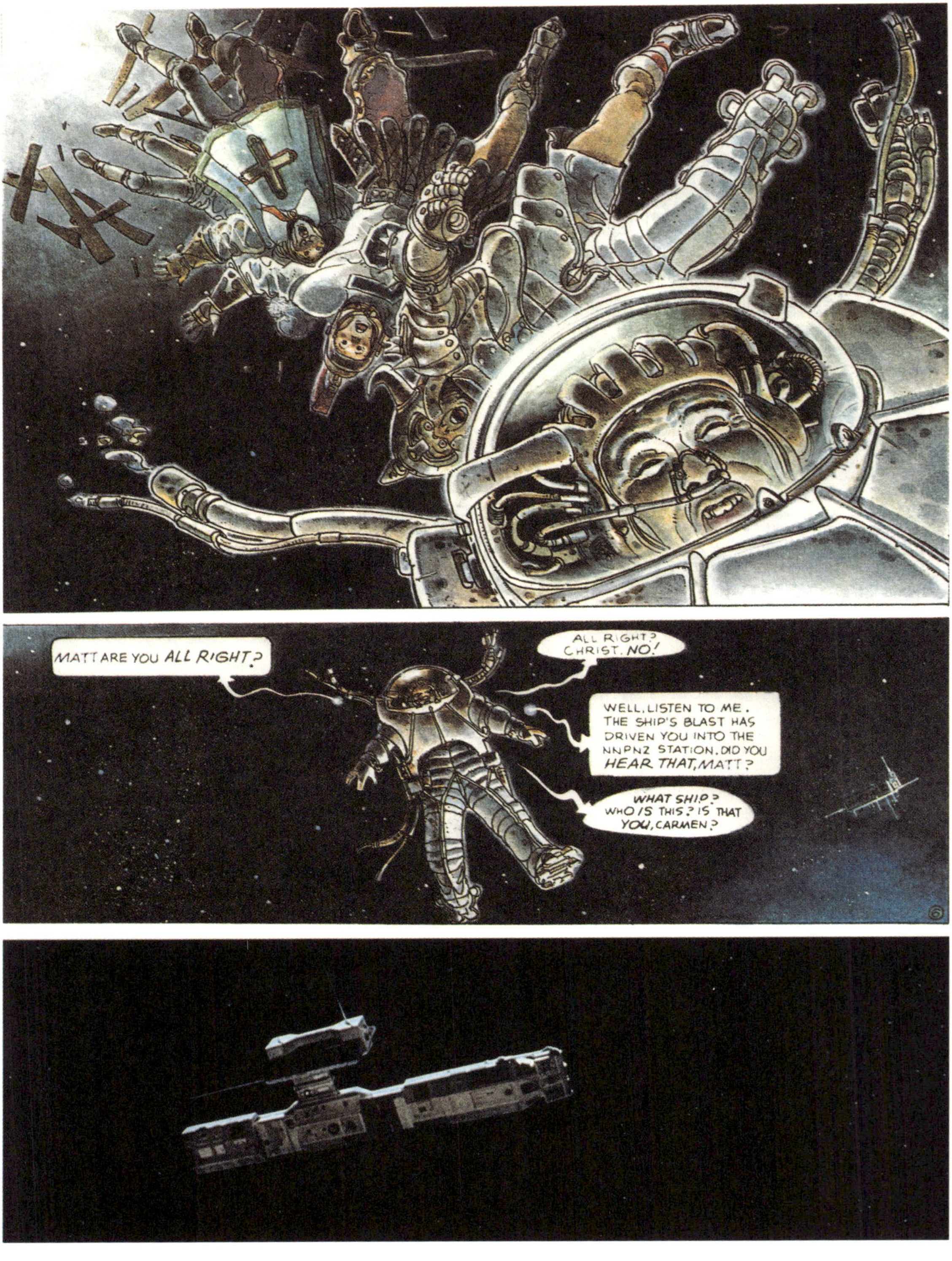
MATT ARE YOU ALL RIGHT?
ALL RIGHT? CHRIST. NO!
WELL, LISTEN TO ME. THE SHIP'S BLAST HAS DRIVEN YOU INTO THE NNPN2 STATION. DID YOU HEAR THAT, MATT?
WHAT SHIP? WHO IS THIS? IS THAT YOU, CARMEN?

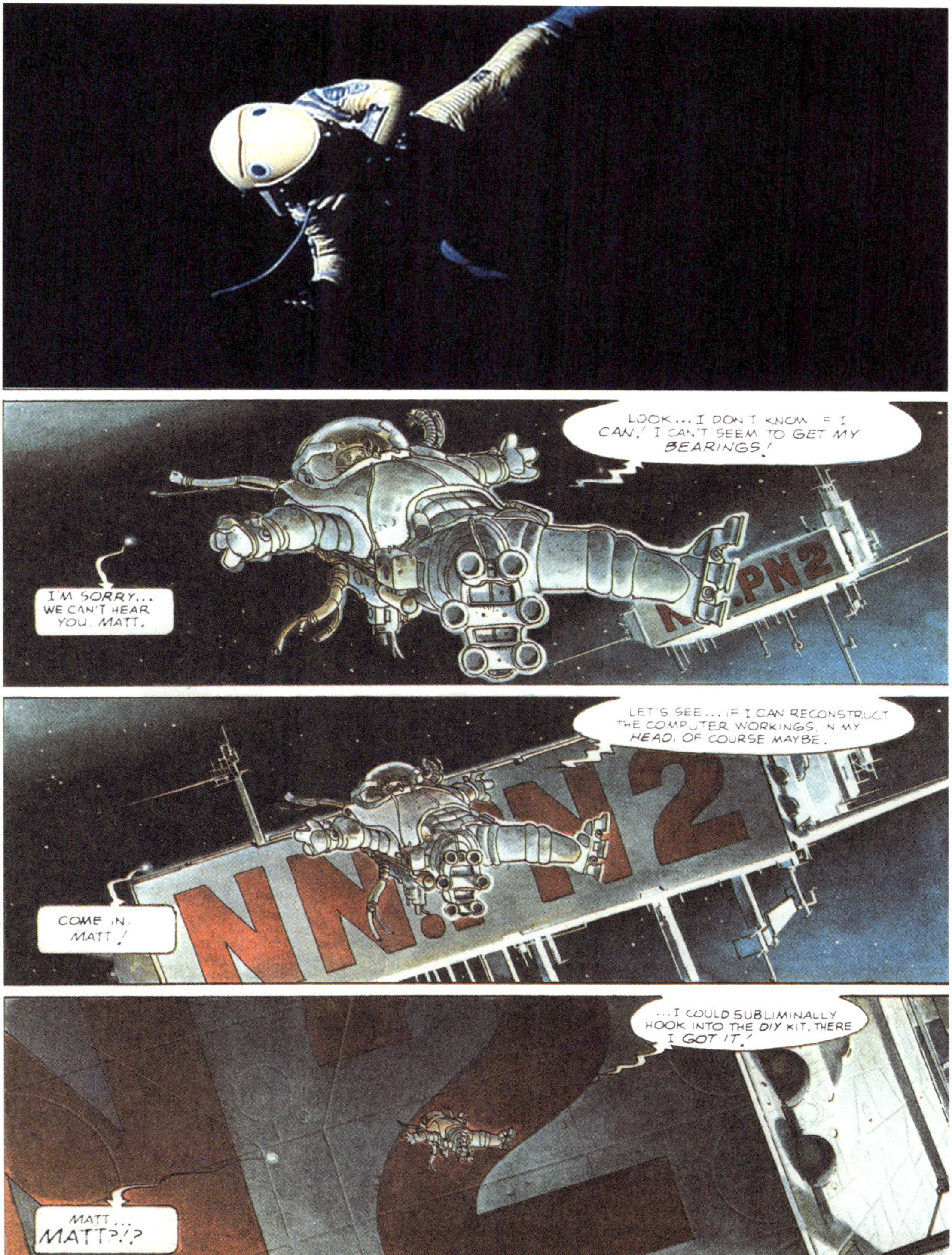
LOOK... I DON'T KNOW IF I CAN! I CAN'T SEEM TO GET MY BEARINGS!
I'M SORRY... WE CAN'T HEAR YOU, MATT.
LET'S SEE... IF I CAN RECONSTRUCT THE COMPUTER WORKINGS, IN MY HEAD, OF COURSE MAYBE.
COME IN, MATT!
...I COULD SUBLIMINALLY HOOK INTO THE DIY KIT. THERE I GOT IT!
MATT... MATT?!?

Li Roos works on Martian land. The Operation Centre relies on her work to calculate the weight of the material and the quality of the vehicular supports. On top of the gravitational force of the place, she also has to test the zones of depression and the zones of hard ground.
She takes advantage of a rare moment of relaxation to read the book found balanced on a dispatch and that no one claims as their own. Stained, damp, its pages glued together, it presents dialogues and images alternatively whose meaning she tries to decipher. A story of a phial which doesn't empty catches her attention.
On top of that, she sees a disturbing connection between the incident which happened on the Cecilia base and the repeated draining occurring in the bunker, on a ship, in a lagoon throughout the various stories. The idea comes into her head that the book has been placed there on purpose by the Operation Centre to test the independent technicians' capacity to explain that draining phenomenon artificially instigated

and planned before the mission. Like an enigma, the book would add some confusion to the whole thing. Li Roos doesn't appreciate in the least that kind of sadistic game or rather that game of supervision of the scientists on a mission. The hierarchy is provoking us, it can't put up with our independent initiatives, even in the name of science. That is what she declares during a snack-break meeting of the whole crew. But her companions don't seem overly affected by her declaration. Tests? No matter! Let's go back to work.

Back to her lab, choosing solitude over that collective cowardice, Roos' thoughts are again taken up by the reticent liquid she read about in the book. If it doesn't flow once the two tips are broken, it's because it's a solid, a jelly, an ultra-light or, much more theoretical: an interface between two realities. Li Roos puts the book down, daydreams while looking at the Martian plain decorated with little slopes and loose stones.≈≈

N O T D R E A M≈

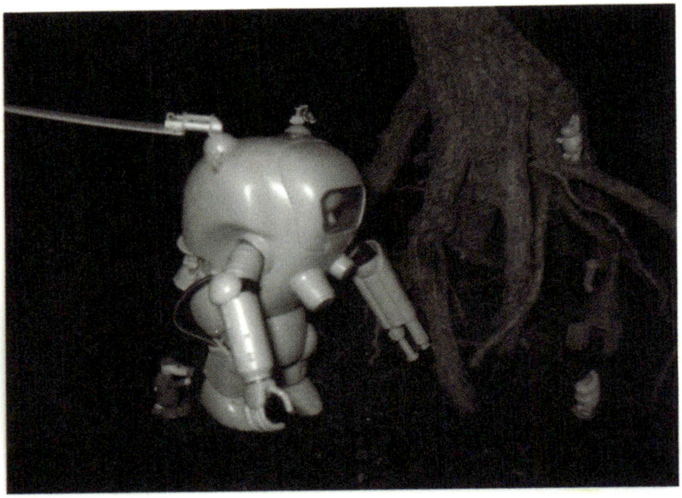

To set time free, to recover the lost men.

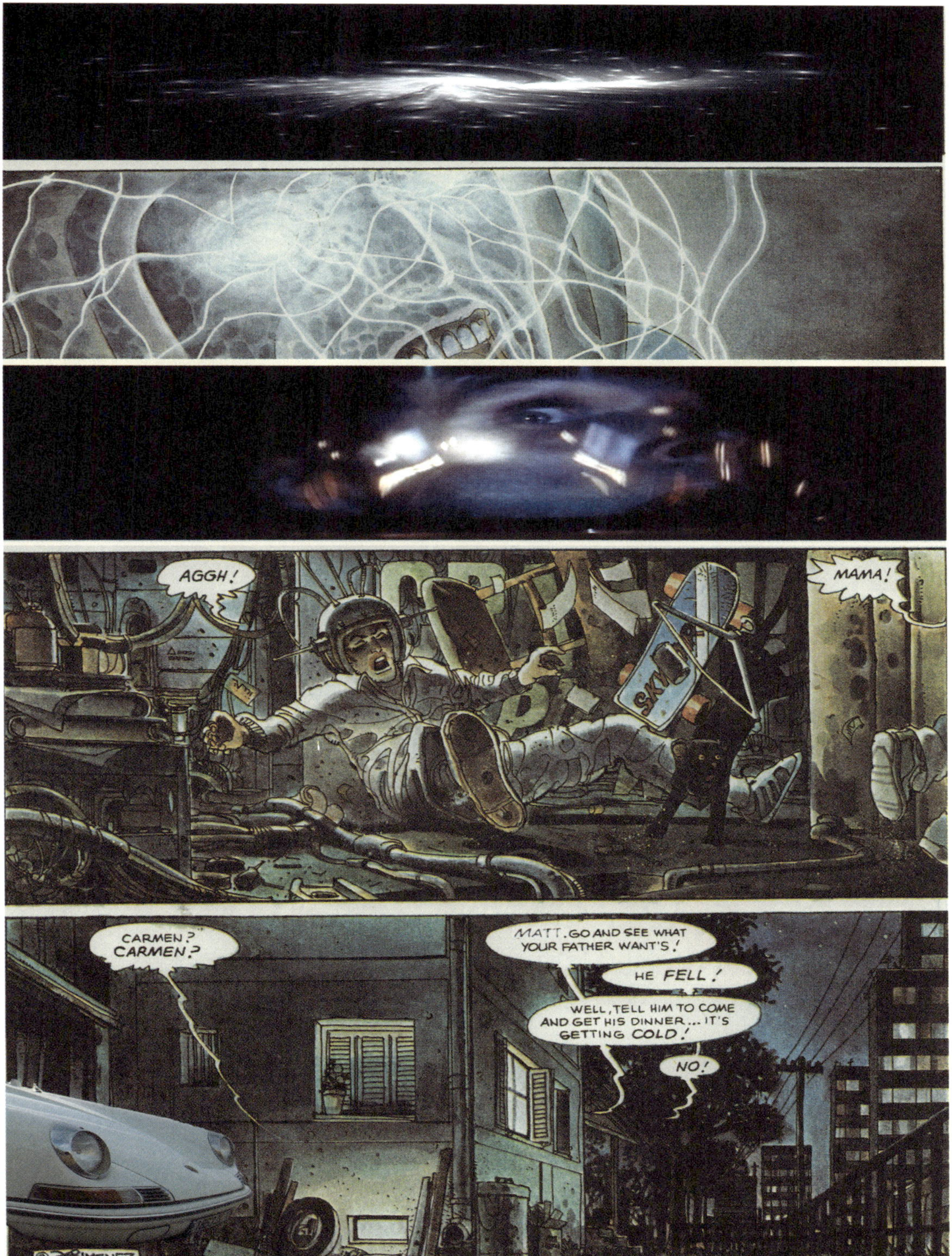
AGGH!
MAMA!
SKY
CARMEN? CARMEN?
MATT. GO AND SEE WHAT YOUR FATHER WANT'S!
HE FELL!
WELL, TELL HIM TO COME AND GET HIS DINNER... IT'S GETTING COLD!
NO!
© JIMENEZ

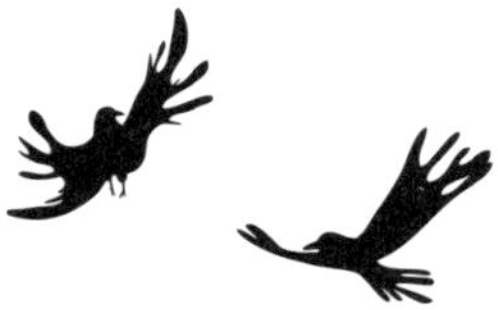

Once your VW is parked, you offer some phials to your friends who seem puzzled.
You tell them where you got your supplies.
They disapprove.
The van you are pointing to is a vehicle for medical emergencies.
The people occupying it are dressed in white blouses.
Locking their van, they join the first techno circles and their dancers.
You force the lock.
You and your friends ransack the shelves until a phial draws your attention.
You grab it, break a tip then the other to allow the contents to flow.
But the liquid remains congealed in its glass phial.
You shake it, wondering about your friend, who also gives it a try.
You take it from his hand and now you have the feeling that the glass is melting.
The phial becomes as liquid as its content.
There, you hurry drinking it, in one gulp.
You slowly leave the van beneath your friend's eyes looking for your first sensations.
You penetrate deep into the forest that borders the clearing.

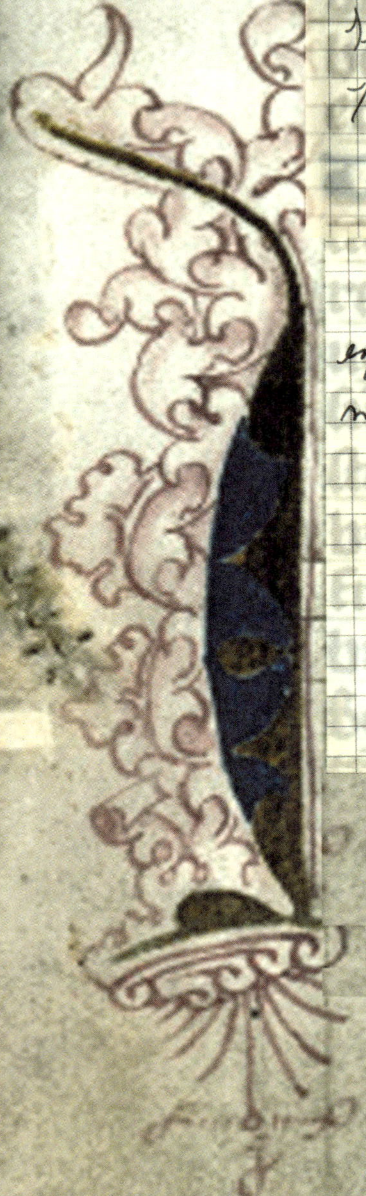

Il y a ce personnage qui lui
se déplace dans l'espace.
Il matérialise la ligne
et répartit un point : ⊢|

Nous créons et diffusons un
espace mental qui tend à pervertir la
notion de réalité.

Rouge.

Reality appears like a concept developed
to create a general cohesion of the whole
of human kind.
But today that concept is under attack,
and it's more and more
clear that it's just an abstraction, and that
reality doesn't exist, and consequently
the original world either.

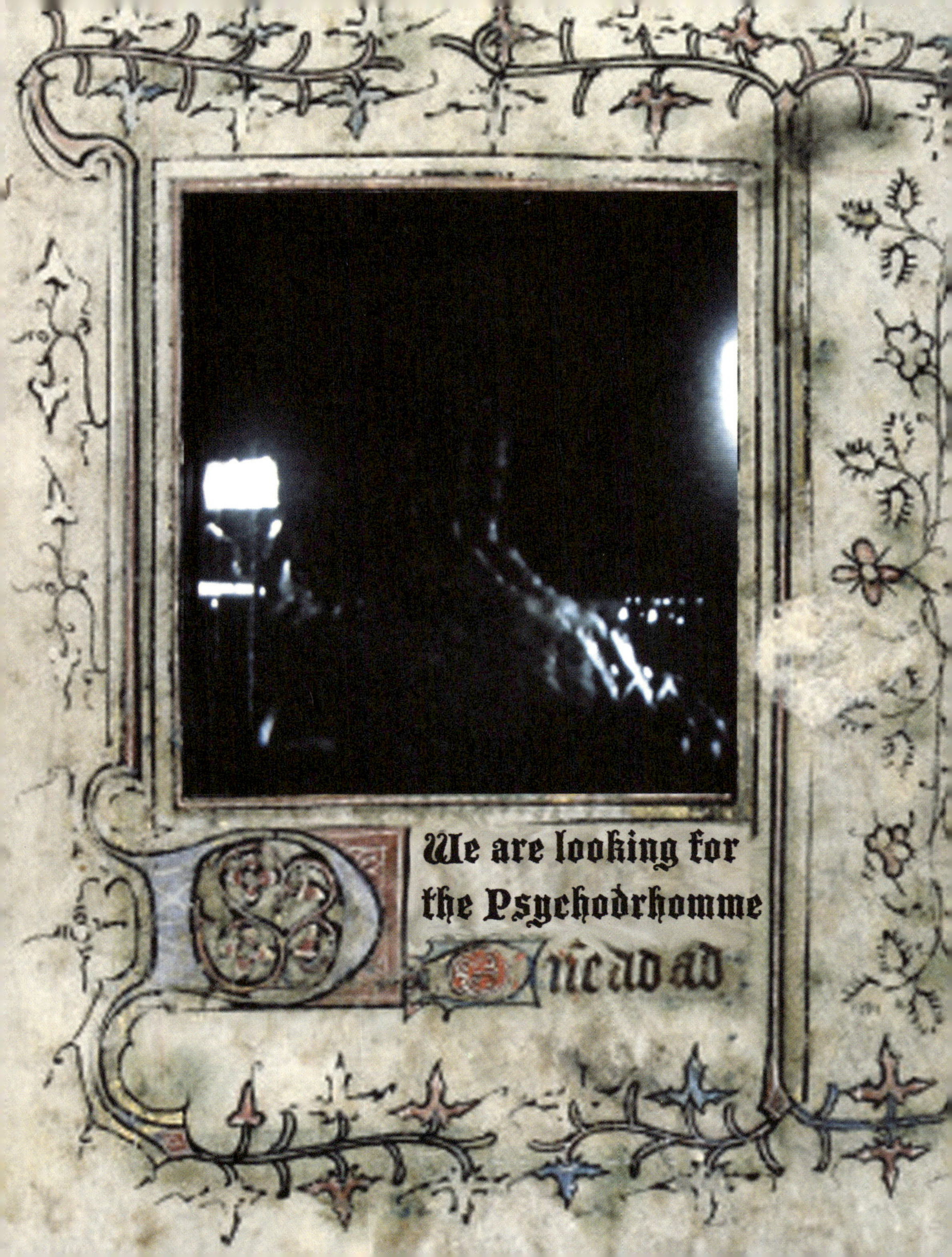
We are looking for
the Psychodrhomme

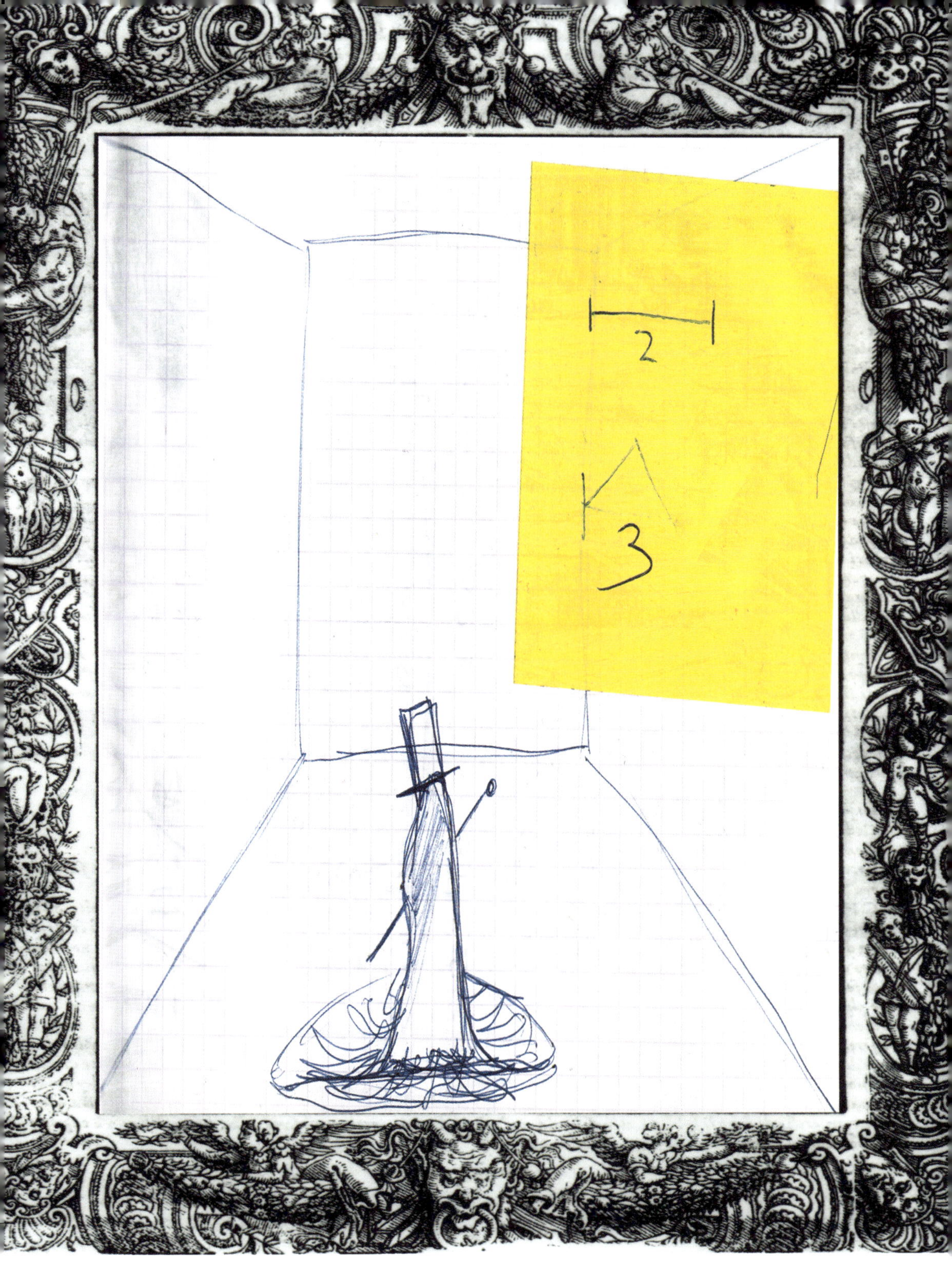
2
3

The next meeting between Lenson and White Wolf is more violent still. When White Wolf points his telescope at the busy ship, he recognizes his prey and immediately opens fire. But if the projectiles miss Lenson's frigate, it's because White Wolf still believes that the exceptional loot accumulated by the runaway is still on board, therefore he wants to scare him, yes, but not sink his ship.

Lenson is not prepared for battle, his cannons are rusty. Keeping fear at bay, the captain contemplates what is so precious on board that White Wolf, the formidable gunman, should deliberately miss his target. He quickly realizes that his pursuer wants to board the ship. Jumping on a barrel, Lenson addresses his crew: White Wolf wants to catch us! He needs something we have! Who can catch our frigate in an open sea race? Who? Hoist up the sails, we're going to win! On those valiant words, the sailors abandon their weapons and cannons to launch their racing ship. After just a few miles at full sail, they notice the three master shrinking on the horizon.

The frigate sails towards the East where a terrible storm catches them unawares. The vessel is badly shaken, struck by rollers, covered in foam. A mast gives way. The following day the ocean is quiet again. Lenson assesses the damage while the sailors try their best to patch together a semblance of bearing. There are still enough sails available but the speed is no longer the same. The white flag with a lion's mouth reappears on the horizon.

White Wolf's ship having ostensibly resisted the storm better is about to catch up with the wounded frigate. The two boats are one mile from each

other, at the most when one of Lenson's lookouts signals coast on the starboard. The captain heads for the coast hoping to find some kind of shelter.
It's a lagoon. Two sandy stretches encircle a circular shallow basin. Convinced that White Wolf is going to catch his ship, Lenson sails into the open lake. Lighter and easier to maneuver, the frigate can pass where the powerful vessel of the predator would surely run aground. The frigate enters, the sailors probe the bed, it's so calm that they can hardly feel the swirl. White Wolf enters the basin too, a few more cable's lengths, and he will board the frigate. His pirates are ready. The ship's draught is more important than Lenson has predicted. It crosses the open lake with no difficulty, sails beyond the border made by the sand bank. The rivals are getting closer. The Cecilists, as they call themselves, are also getting ready to fight.
Suddenly, the basin's water flows back into the ocean with a swiftness that surprises the two vessels. Lenson feels his frigate rising a little, while his pursuer's ship swivels around with no reason until one of the pirates cries out: we're aground, we're aground! The ship's draught had shrunk three good meters in a few seconds. This time White Wolf is stuck.
Noisy relief takes hold of the frigate's crew. Songs, laughter and sarcastic encouragements accompany one of the sailor's proposition: to crown the flowing lagoon, Philly's lock!

NOT DREA M

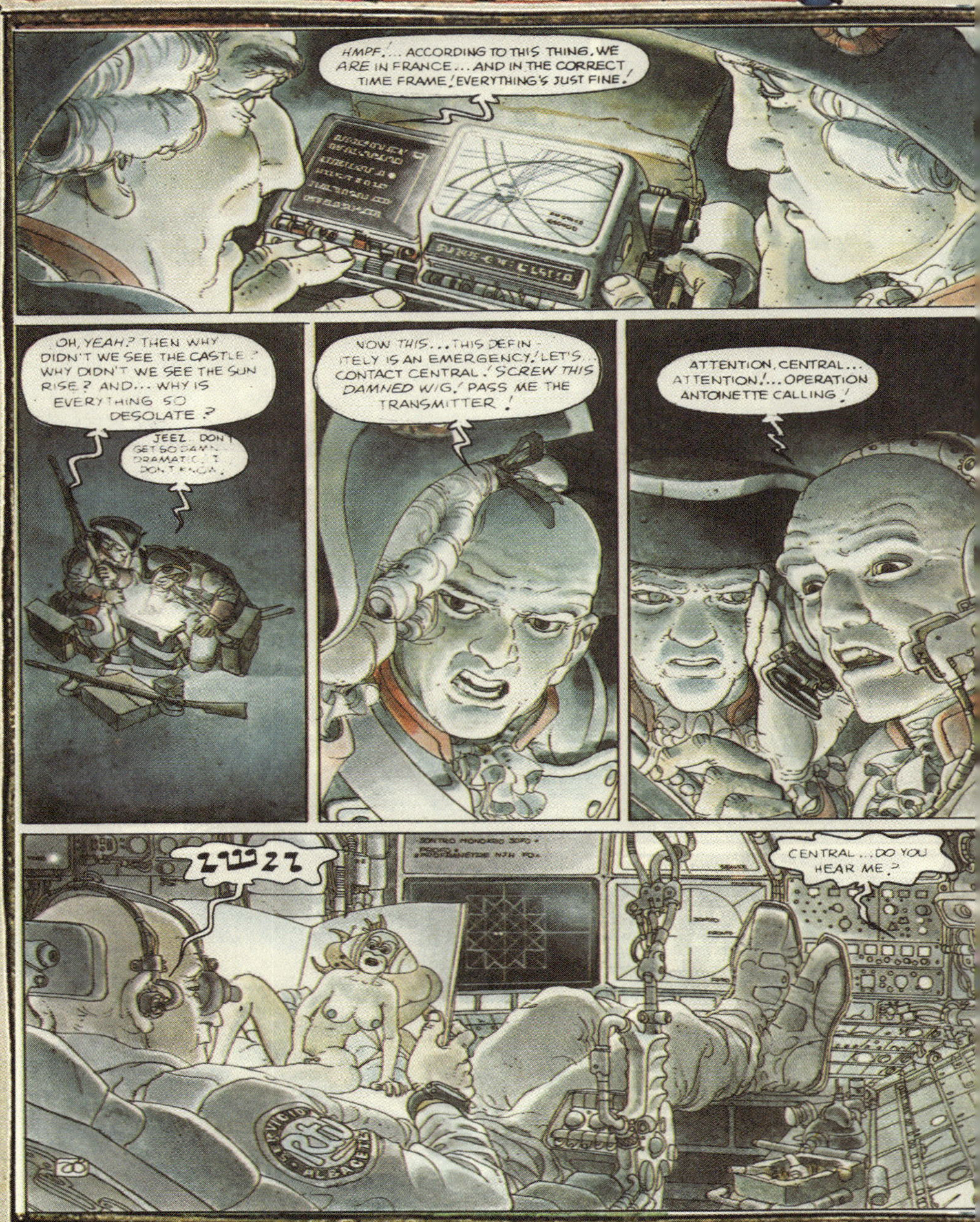

We send our clones through time.

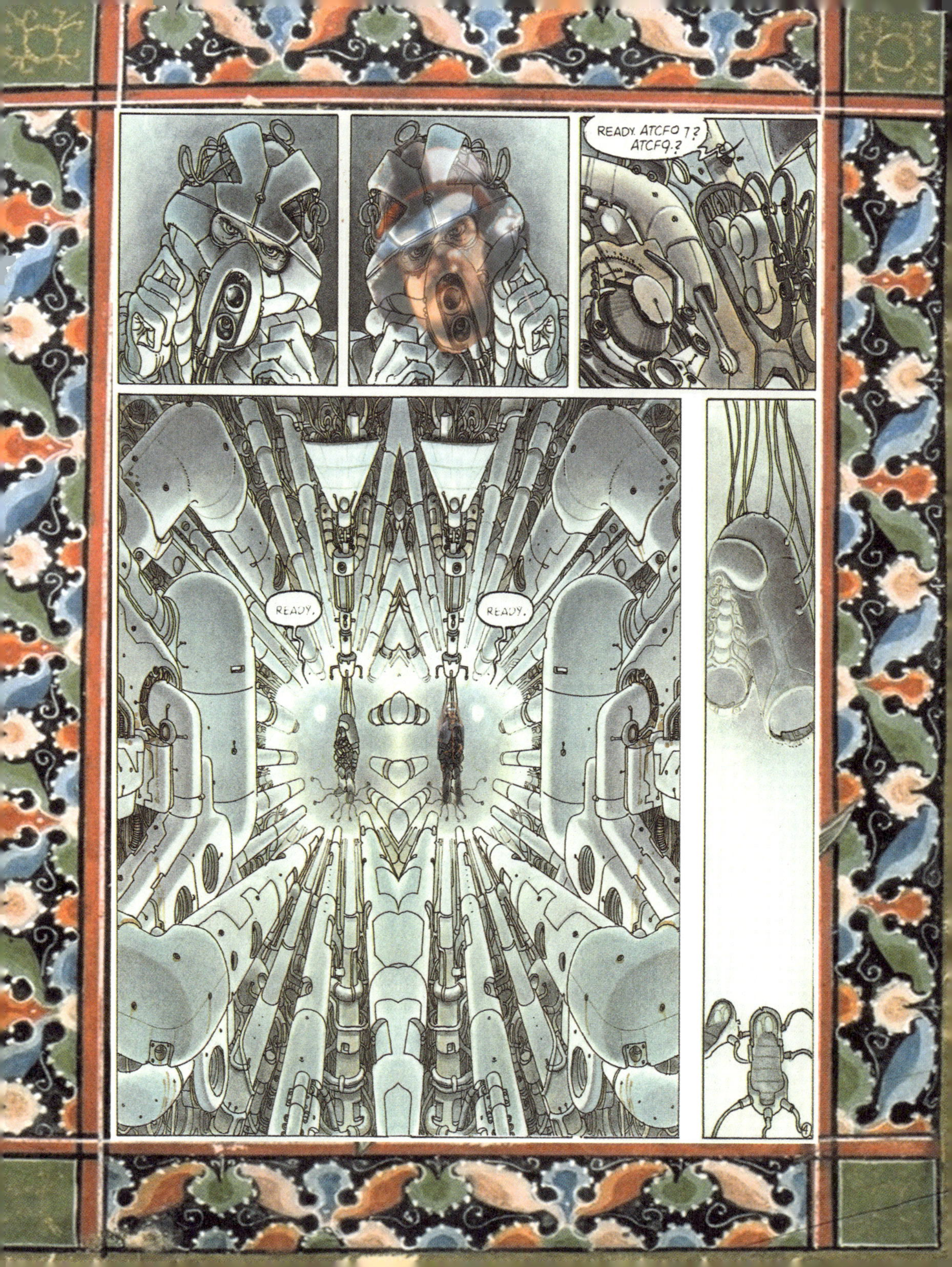
READY. ATCFO 7?
ATCF9.?
READY.
READY.

You plunge deep into the forest that borders the campsite.
You come across your twin, looking frightened, who appears to go in search of help.
You want to understand, you call him, he trips on a root, you think you can catch him.
He's already near the VW, much calmer now, focused on the words spoken by his friend who holds a book firmly.
Look at that, Matt:
5. Mark H. Simmons interprets that image of the wolf as a reminiscence. Not a personal memory, but a collective one. The memory of an animal origin, the long chain of reminiscences which brought out the individual. What we've kept from the herd, the hordes and packs, what we've gained in independent humanity, machine contraption, guardian machines, technology. The shadow is a tribute, the three-dimensional body, hominization and sovereignty.

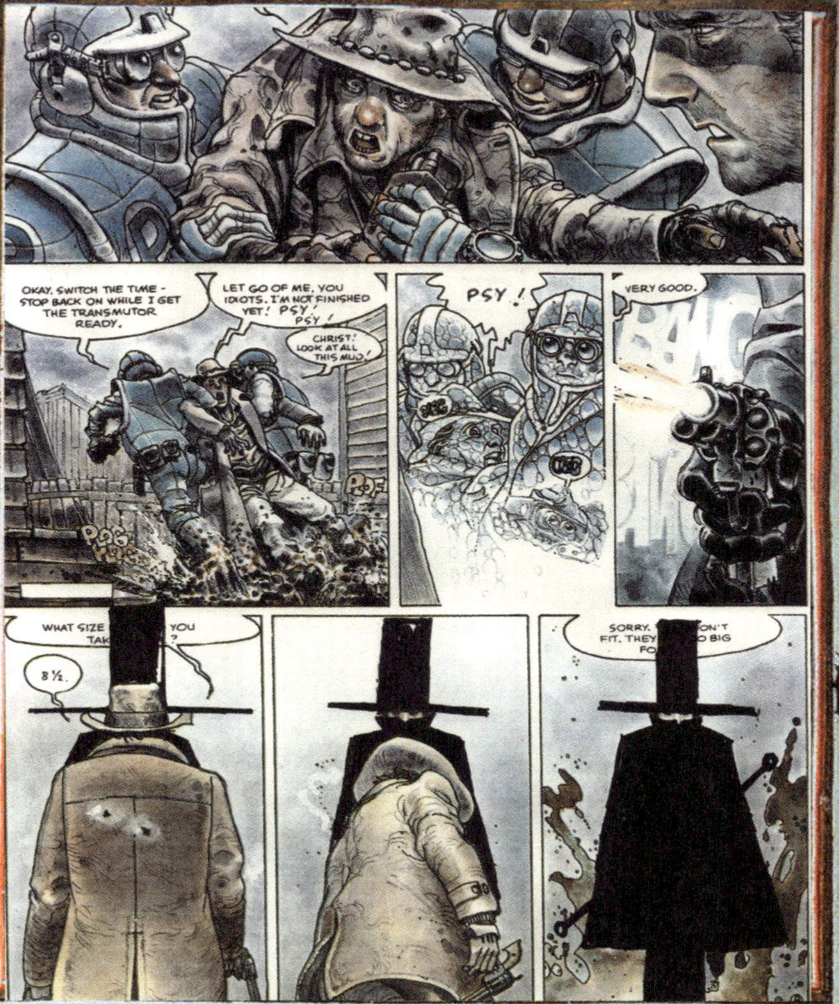

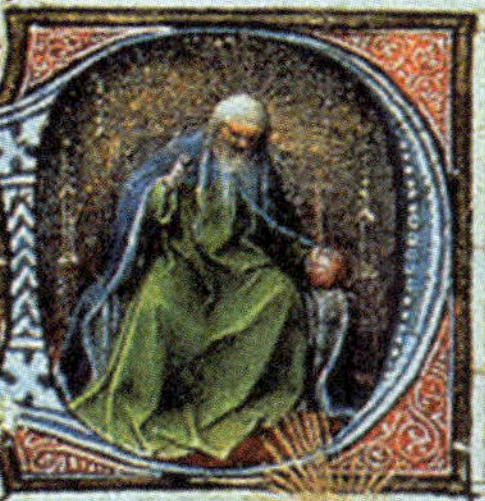

But sometimes they leave the rails
and we have to intervene
and sometimes even eliminate them, if the
psychodrhomme hasn't done it already.

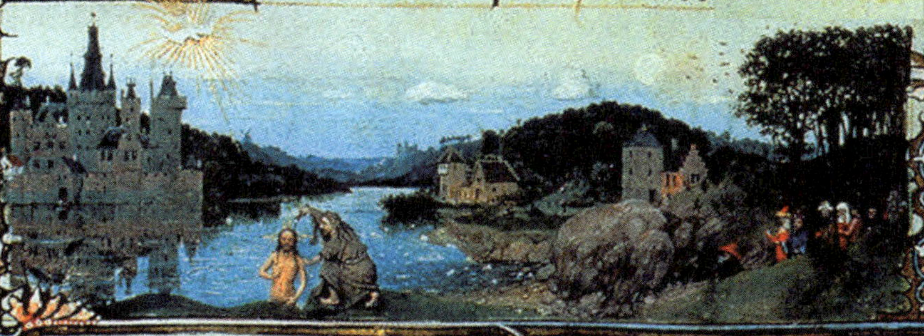

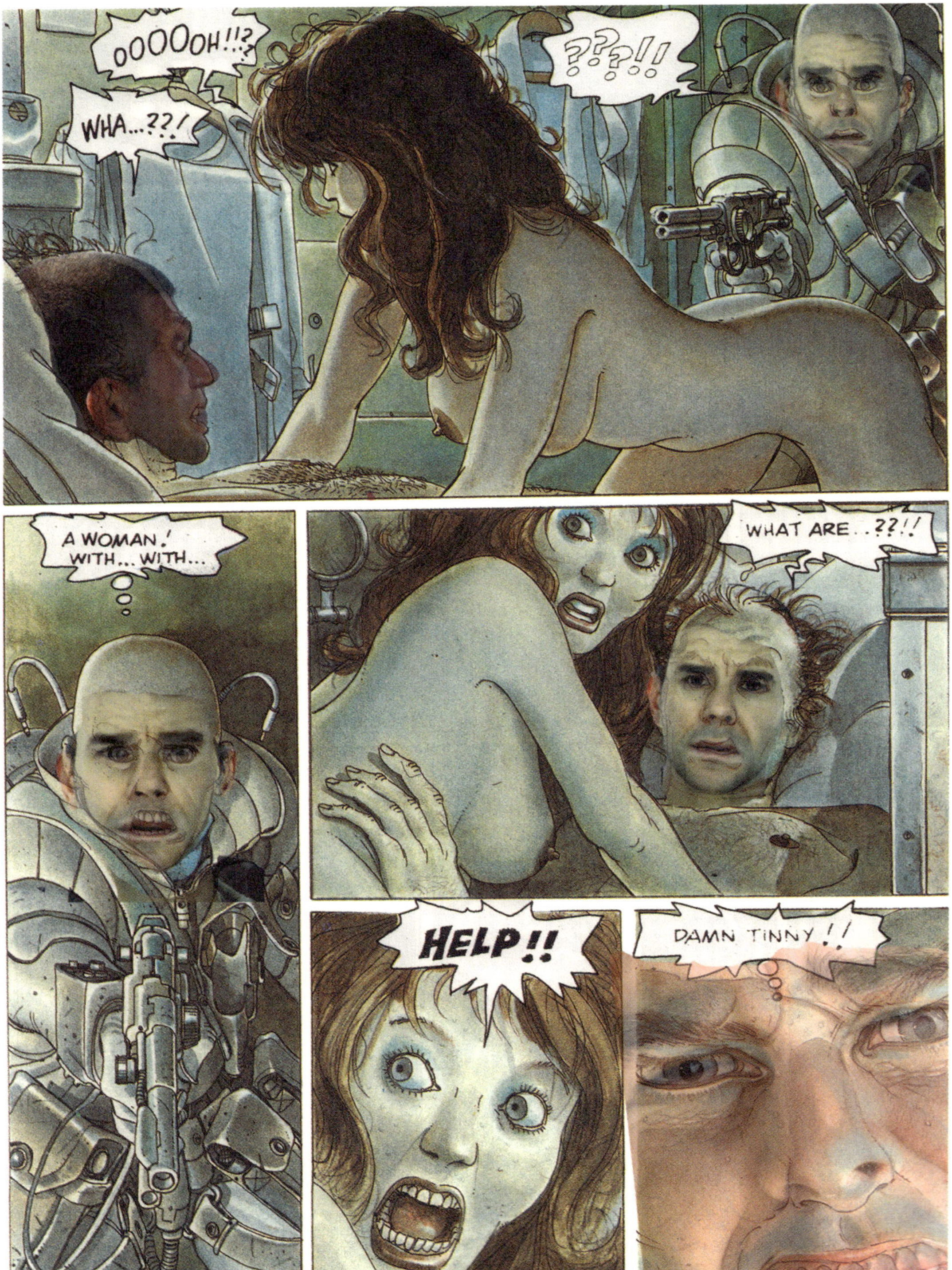
OOOOOH!!?
WHA...??!
??!!
A WOMAN! WITH... WITH...
WHAT ARE..??!!
HELP!!
DAMN TINNY!!

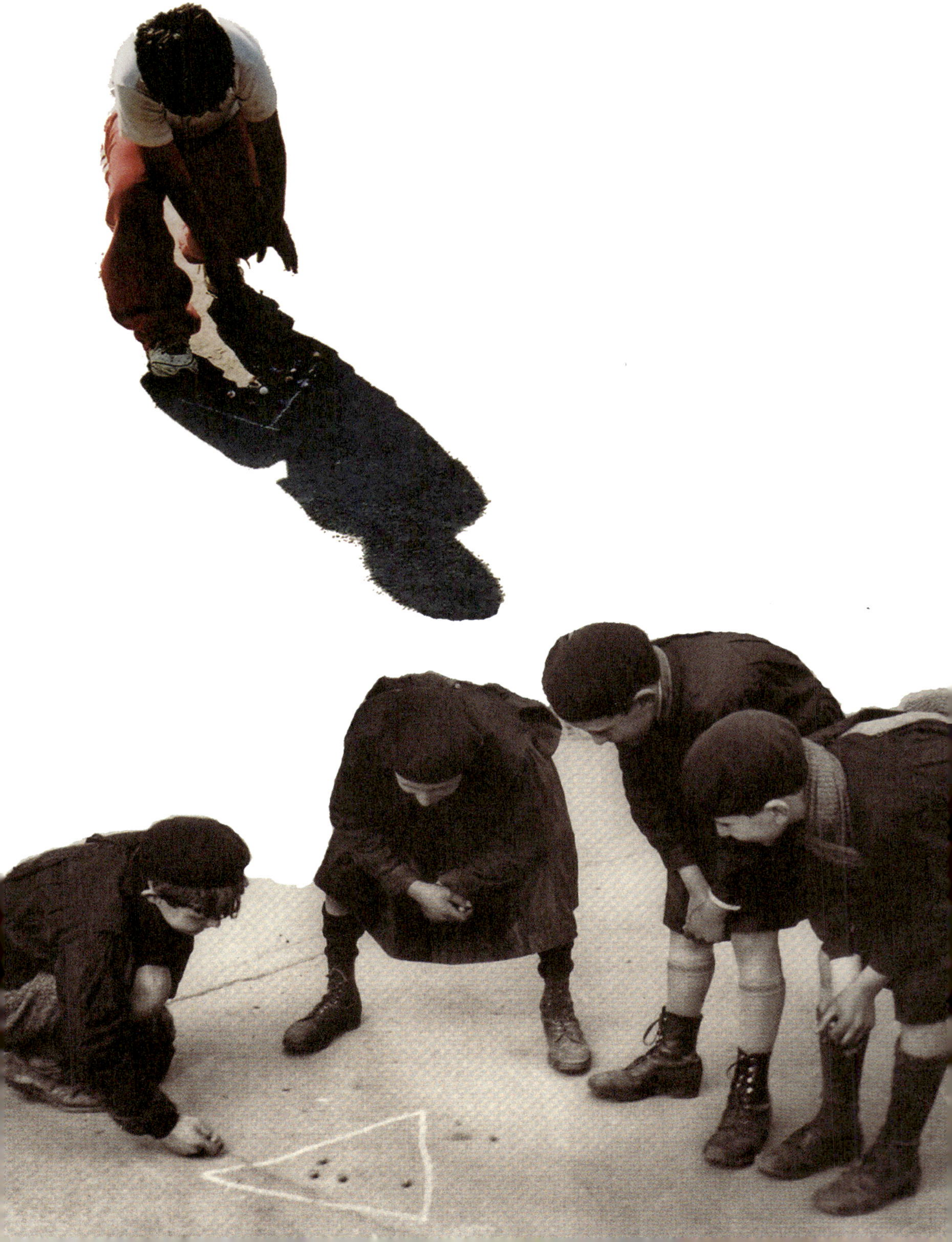

– déplacement du centre.

L'île est elle le centre quand on la vise. comment l'espace s'articule t-il face à un point. Et le temps ?

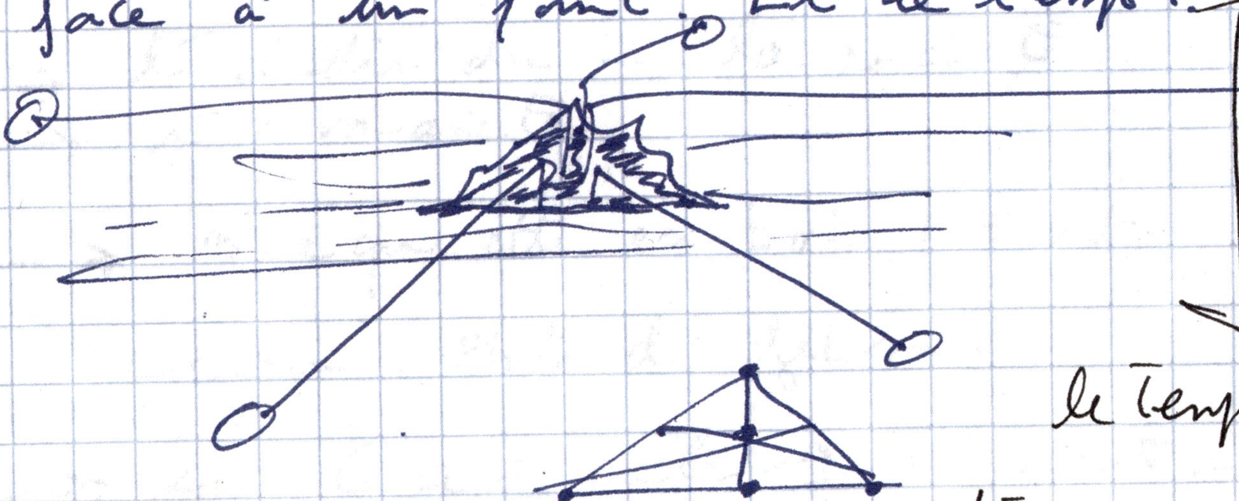

le temps c l'axe

l'axe courbe ?

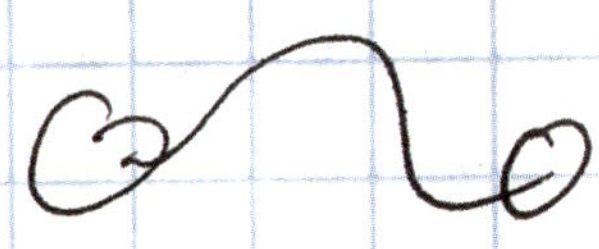

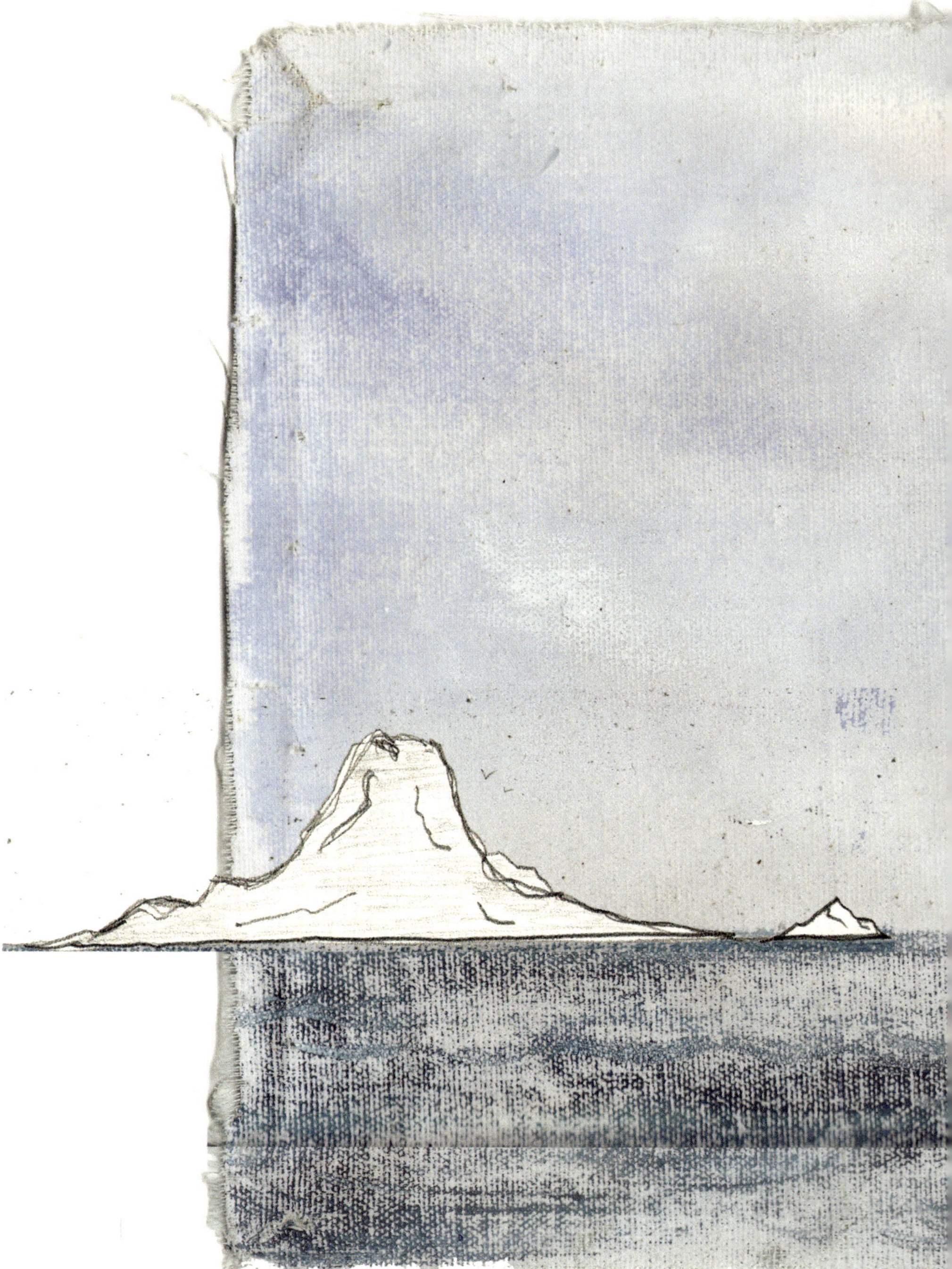

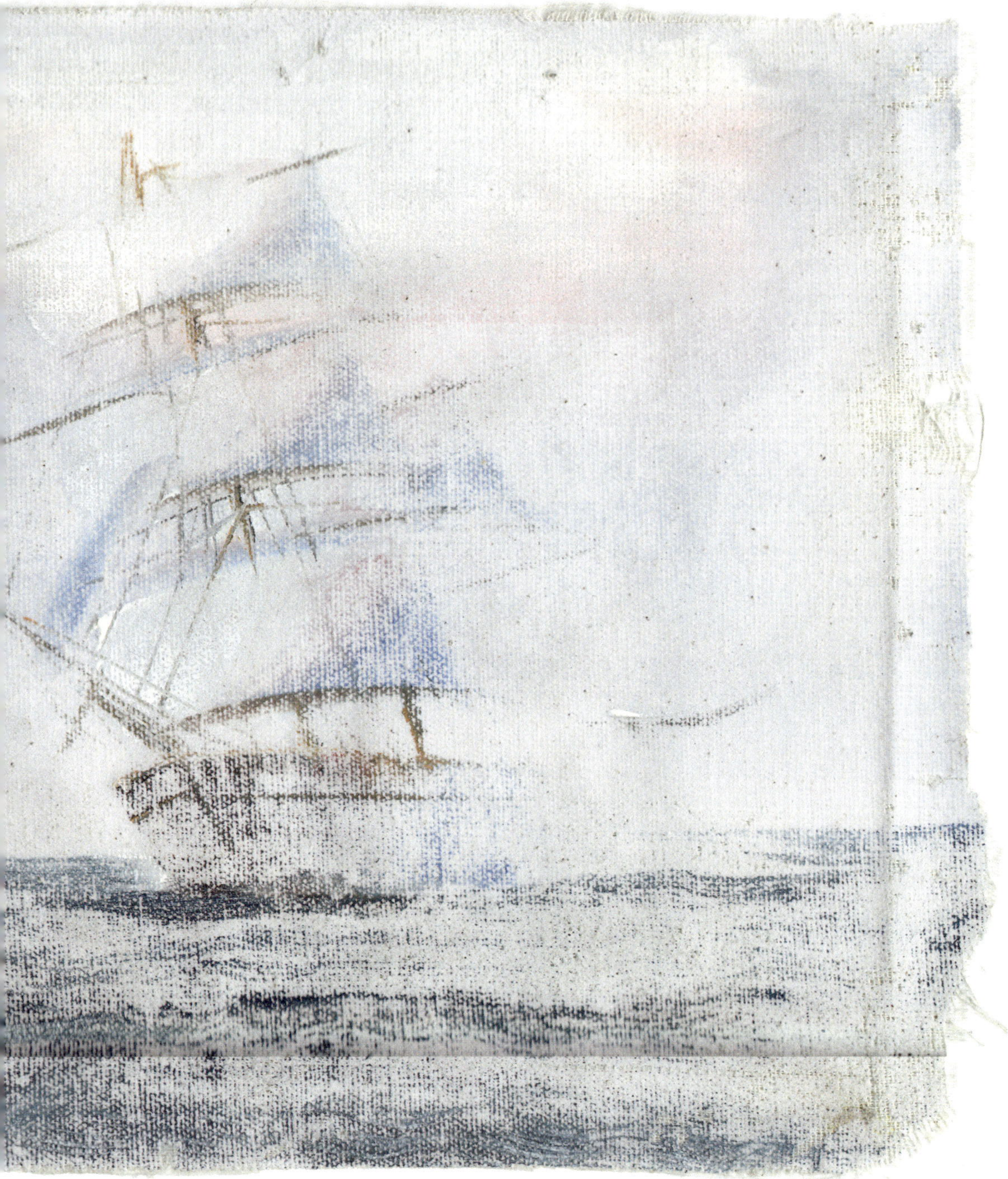

Lenson's frigate is serenely sailing due East, direction Cape Town. The sailors are starting to get restless, anxious about the lack of food available on board. Fishing is mere chance, as is an encounter at sea. The lookouts scrutinize the horizon, eager to make an announcement. Lenson gives advise to his crew of free men, a compass clutched in his hand. An idea comes to his head that to be a captain at sea, a respected captain whose choices are wise and bold, won't do any good once the colony is settled. If their ideal of a libertarian society was going to be realized, what use would his reputation be as pilot? And what worth would be their ideal if his men made him responsible for the harvest, village chief or charismatic leader. The unpredictable ocean imposes its hierarchy, and shortage of supplies on board could impose its own crisis.

Cape Town! The lookout is jumping up and down on his perch. He has seen the imposing mass of the immense mountain which announces the Cape of Good Hope and its adjoining city.

Lenson and his relieved crew enter the harbor where the ships are far and few. Some trawl nets, a vessel unloading its spices, a brick from the English navy but, above all, a wreck which intrigues the captain enormously. A frigate has run aground in the channel. Its distinctive shape is still visible but shells have already colonized the deck. Spending the following night at the Tetrahedron tavern, its name coming from the geographical form of its sign, Lenson sketches on a board the draft for an imaginary vessel inspired by the dream he had on the island. It's a three-master to which he adds the masts as well as a complete set of sails. He calls it Psychodrhomme, like the name adopted by the chief of the tribe. He makes up a bill of purchase connected with the plans, then registers the document at the counter. Returning to his frigate, he approaches the wreck to which he gives his ship's name. It has the letters of a half-visible name carved on the hull: Libert'.

His companions appreciate the maneuver: to convince the pursuers that Libertalia has run aground here, that the captain and his crew have bought another ship containing the mythical loot, and that this new crew is heading for Madagascar. After taking on fresh supplies, the real frigate steers to the South to resume its journey West, direction Argentina and Cecilia.

A few weeks later, White Wolf's vessel is moored at Cape Town. The pirate is trying to figure out if Lenson's frigate has come here, and it's at the Tetrahedron's counter that he is given some information. The runaway has taken possession of a three master that was on sale in the harbor, these are the plans. He is transporting his huge freight of chests to Madagascar. White Wolf gives his sailors a day off to rest, before resuming his pursuit, searching for a three-master called Psychodrhomme, that is reputed to be slower. In the bay, they come across what's left of a frigate floating under water. The wreck is greeted with enthusiastic and sarcastic cheers.

D REAM

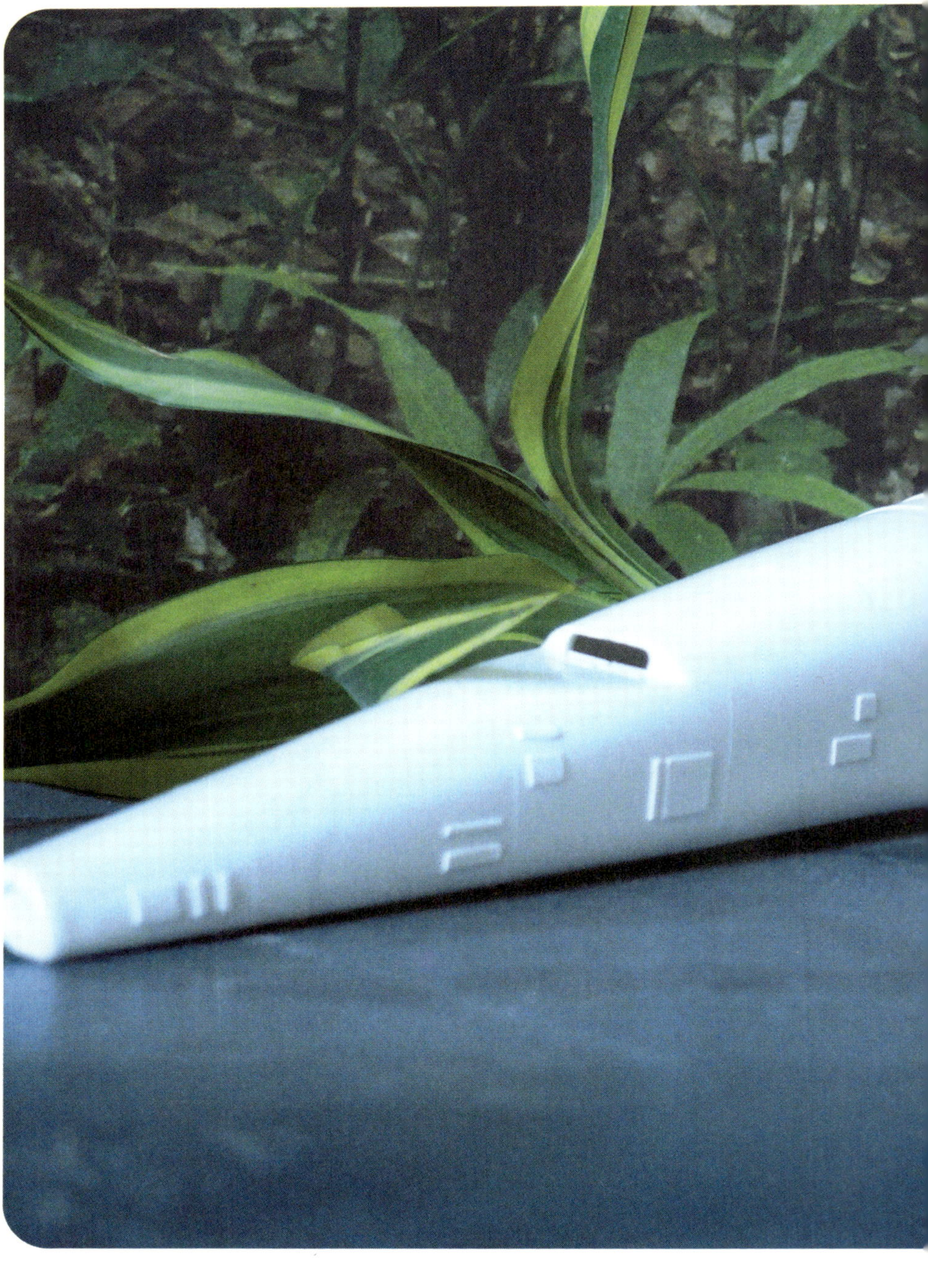

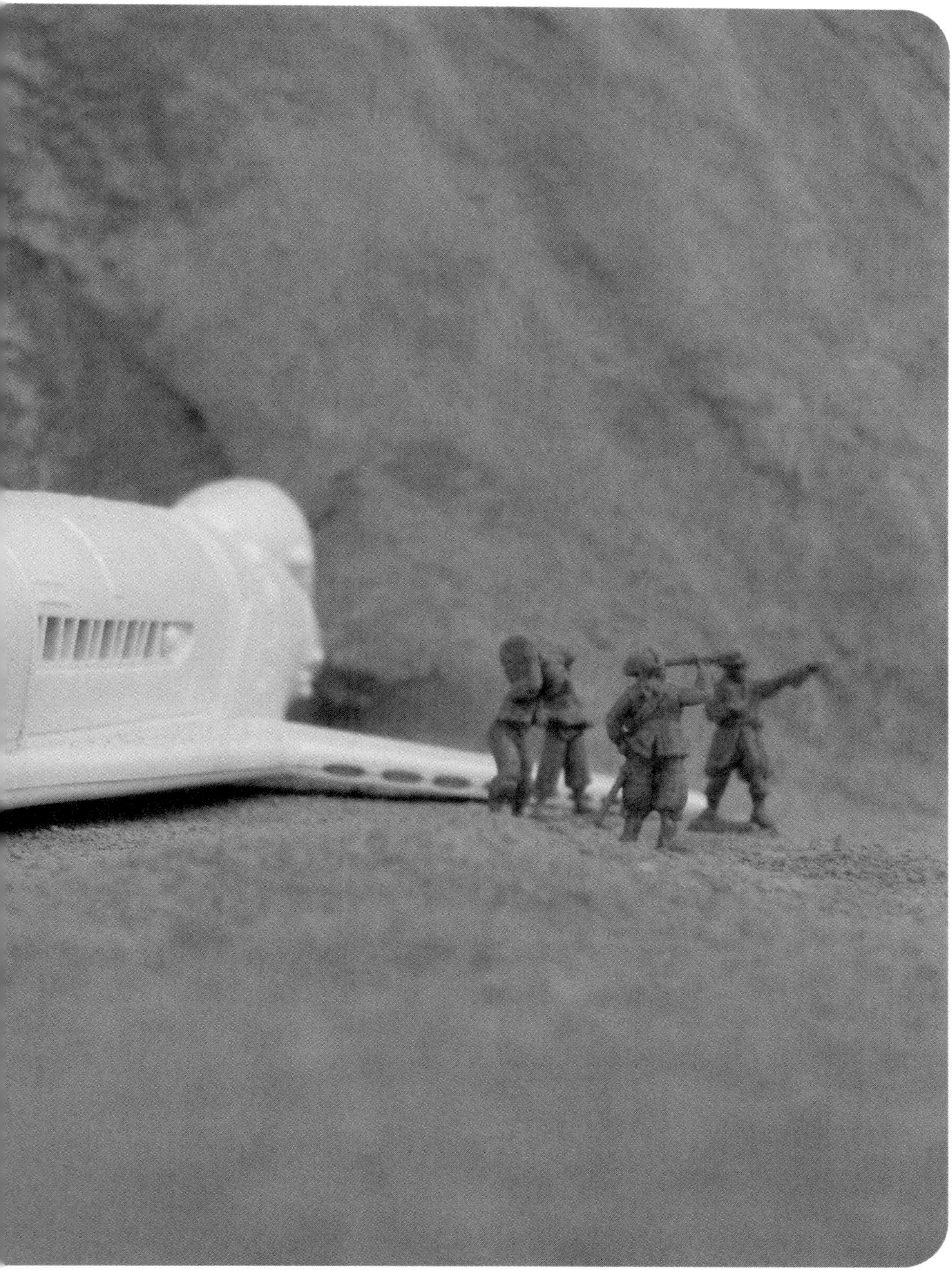

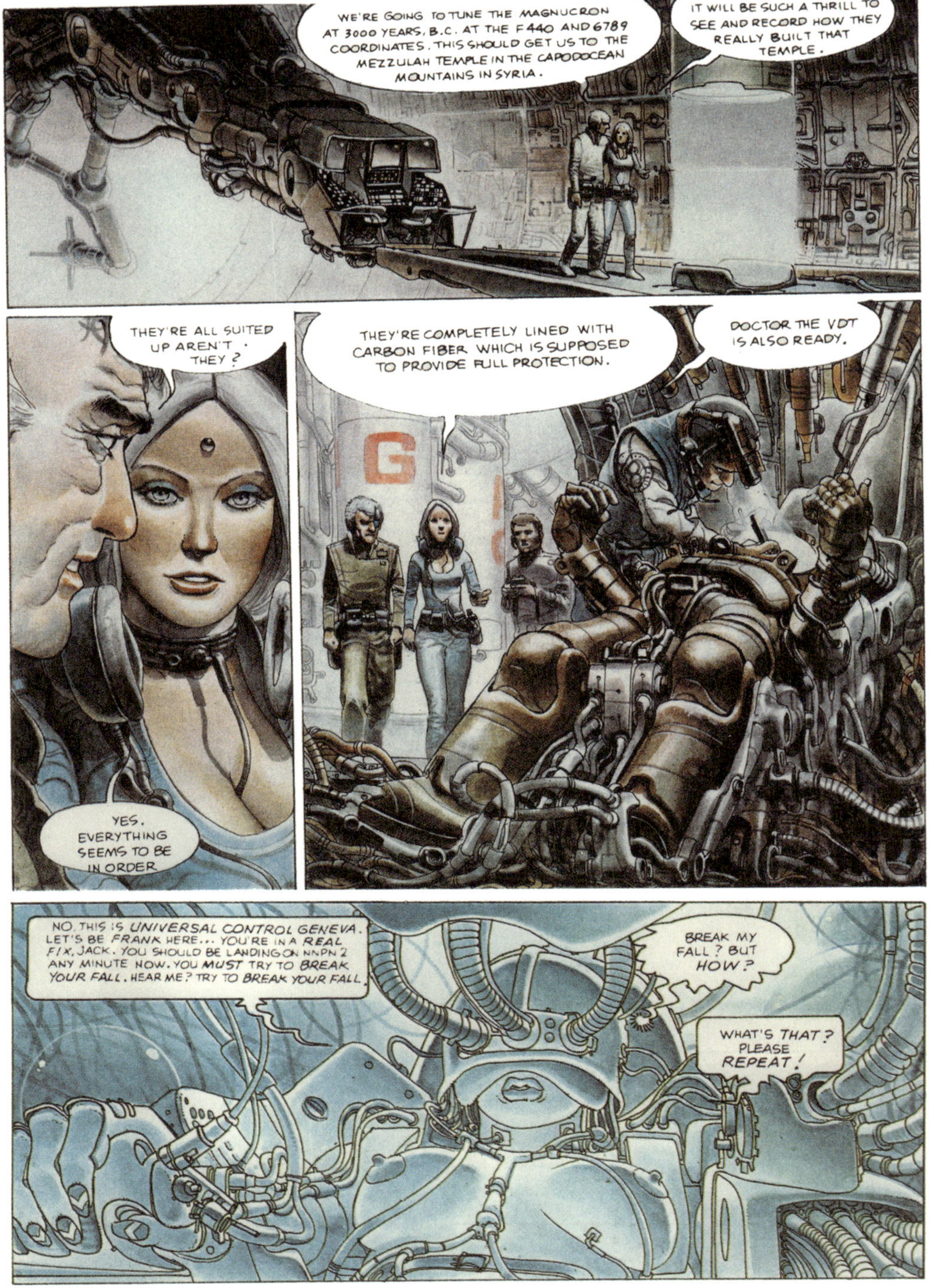

We have to intervene. For the fact of crossing from the original world to the world of synthe
through non-controlled means corrupts the original world and plunges its population
into an uncontrollable schizophrenia. Between the two, the infra-slim deteriorates.

You woke up.
You slipped into your boiler suit and you wait till the water rises in the bunker.
Enough for you to be able to dive in with your whole body.
This boiler suit is therefore amphibious.
1m 50, you dive.
You dive.
You find yourself in an over-equipped lab, in front of a half-open airlock.
The landscape is a plain of loose stones, lit by an oblique light.
Another person wearing the same suit with a helmet says: shall we go?
You answer: Okay, but once at point B, we have a break, like we said.
He answers: like we said.
On the path, you take a few samples of minerals, and so does your colleague.
Both squatting, observing the samples, your colleague asks you: what did you do originally?
You reply, puzzled: originally?

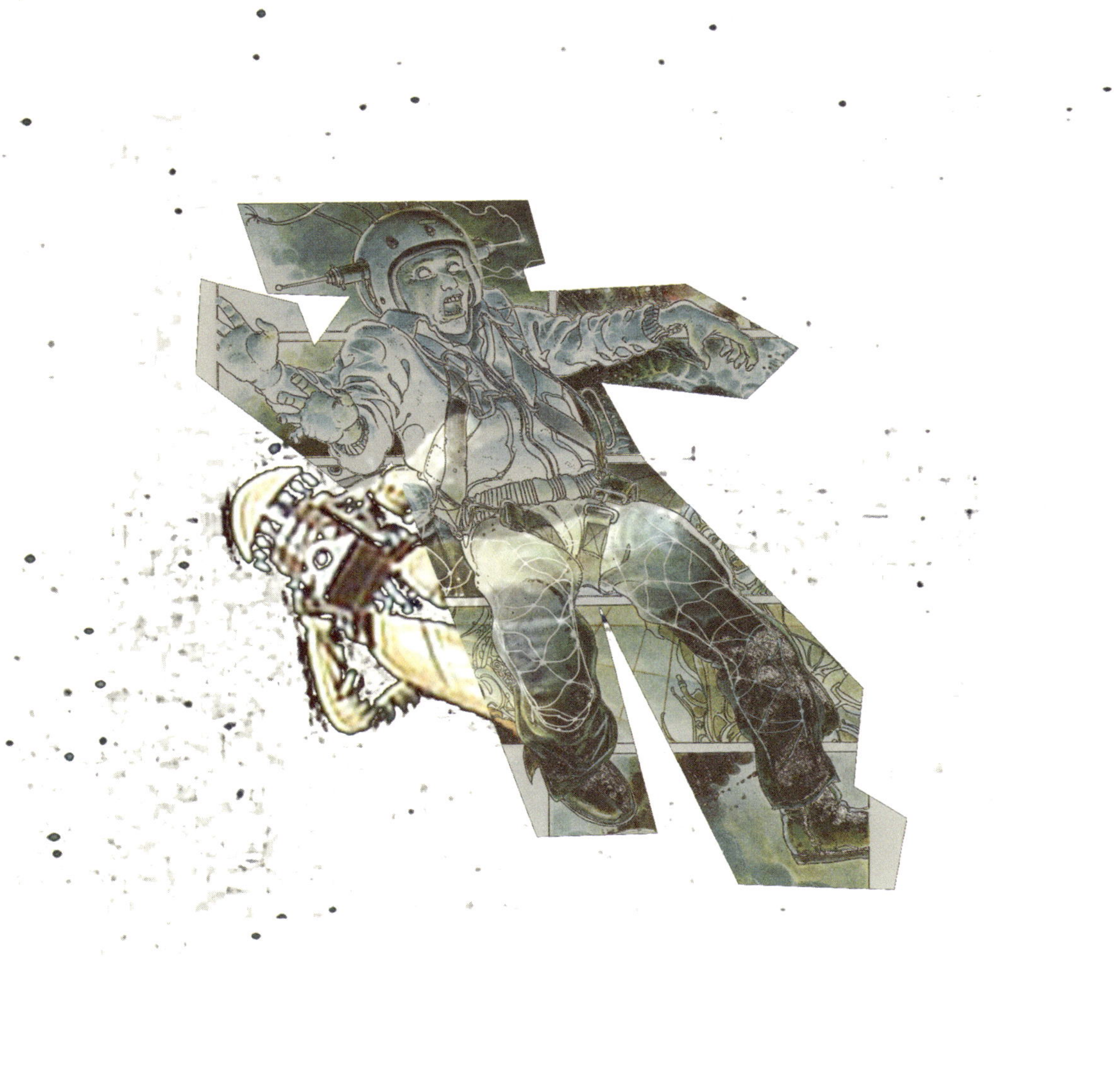

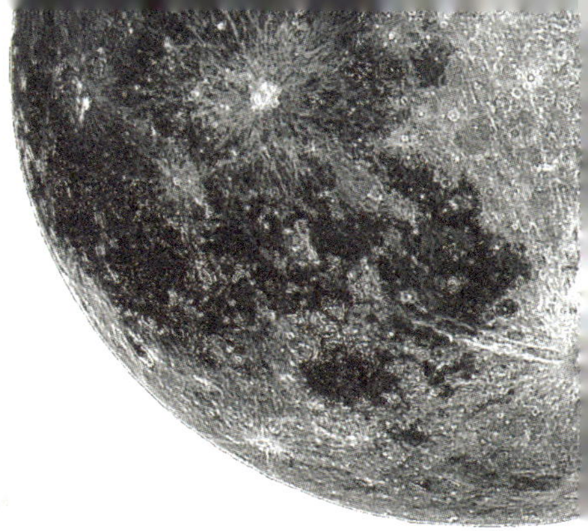

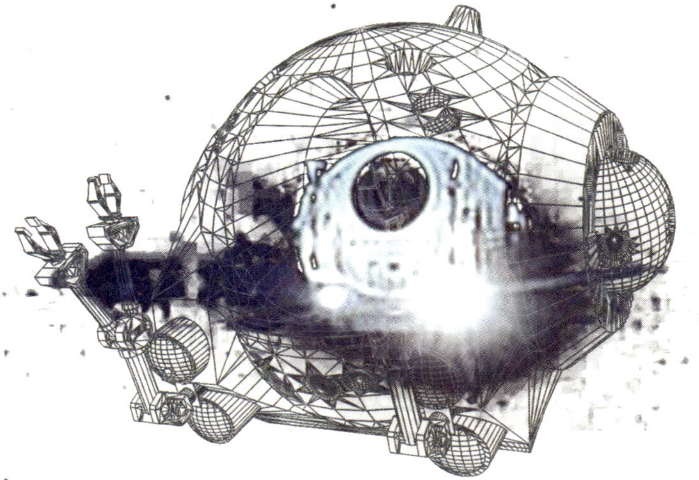

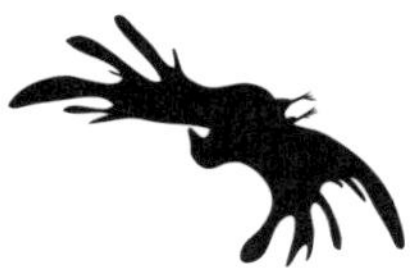

You colleague says: we could take off our helmets if we wanted.

What?

Yes, reread the line KZ/LZ/020: we are made to sustain Martian air.

I haven't seen that passage.

I've seen it.

If you say so. But I'm not removing my helmet right in the middle of a mission.

Okay, but you could do it.

I won't do it.

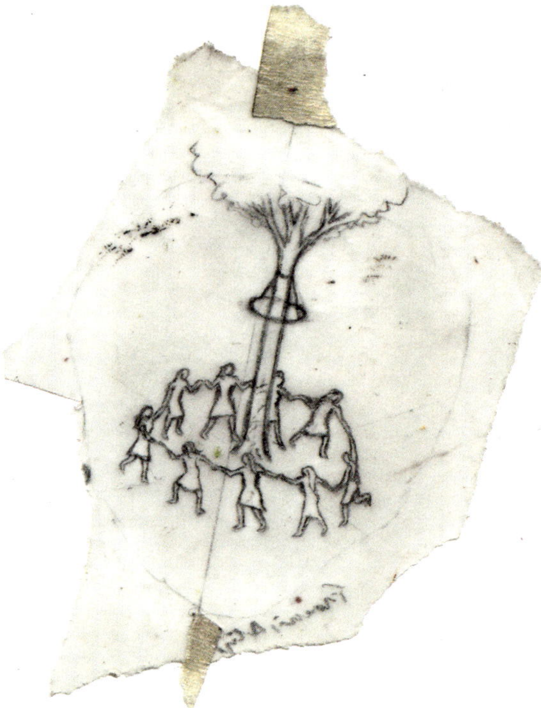

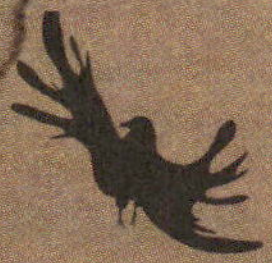

Mark, look, the door has been broken!
Shit, the handle's stuck.
Psycho, come and see, someone has broken into the van.
Told you, one of us should've stayed in it.
The phials, they have ransacked the phials but didn't take any.
Didn't take any?
The drug squad, you think?
No, it's not their method.
Who, then?
You're going to know very soon: they drunk the pod.
What's that?
A XP phial, let's just say, loaded, very loaded. You can spot the person who took it straight away. The pod has its user think that his capacity for movement is ultra fast, as if he could access a menu where he could suddenly change location or time according to his desire. The problem is that to control the journey requires some training. The person who dives in too quickly soon experiences a feeling of panic, faced with the changes in location, which are as random as they are violent. The druggy can often be found lying around uncomfortably in the middle of the technoïd noise, trying to sleep in order to free himself from the nightmare.
Let's go and look for him then.
This time, Mark, you stay here.

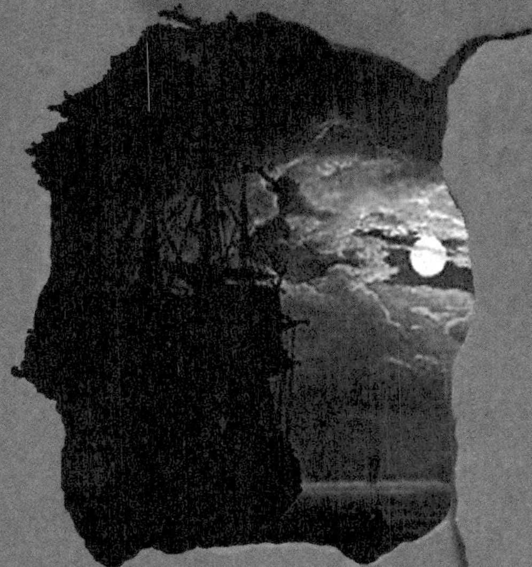

As for Lenson, he is on his way to Argentina, and his crew is back to its own cheerful self. Seeing the green coast leading to Cilia Bay, each companion silently experiences the joy of return, as if they were expected, as if that Cecilia, free of all dwellings, was their native land. Some can see themselves tracing the foundations on the ground: square, rectangular, isosceles triangle and red circle. Others bring back trunks to carve doors, floor, windows; others still sow seeds, weave nets, speak their minds. Cecilia virtually takes shape as the frigate throws anchor one mile from the coast, for the sea is very rough.

The boat carrying Lenson and ten scouts draws near the beach. They can see seats of fire, a few basic constructions, two or three men busy re-erecting a partition wall. At the place itself, where they had marked out their settlement, some colonizers, sardine fishermen most probably, had taken the place.

Without introducing himself, Lenson asks to see the village chief, while the locals just realize a ship has arrived near their beach. A crowd forms around the sailors, who find compatriots amongst them.

The village chief, White Wolf himself, slightly shrunk with age, blunt and calm, walks towards a bewildered Lenson.

A long silence weighs on that encounter. The villagers, the scouts and the sailors who have remained on the frigate look at each other, slightly anxious, in a torpor only interrupted by White Wolf's dry remark:

So you are the one chasing me now, are you, Lenson?

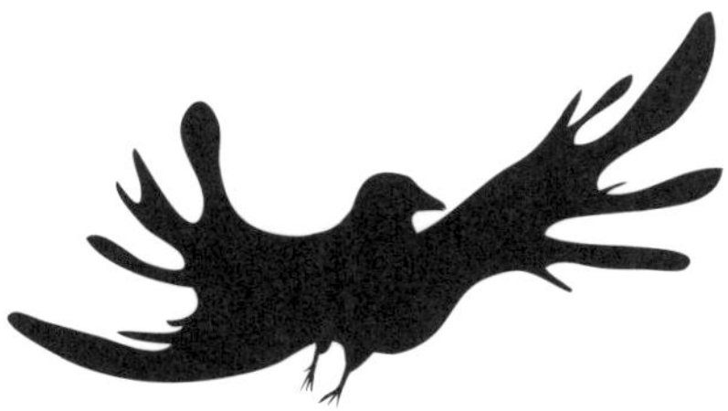

Hey, Psycho, the XP phial, what was it doing in our stuff?
I wanted to try it one more time.
Have you tried it already then?
Yeah, I was even the first to ever try it. I still remember the first effects. The water gave me the feeling of time travel, while the air let me experience a geographical journey, and what was floating, the intersection of the two, served as a bridge.
A bridge to where, for example?
I don't know: a ship, a barrel, a raft…
And did you travel a lot?
Not enough.

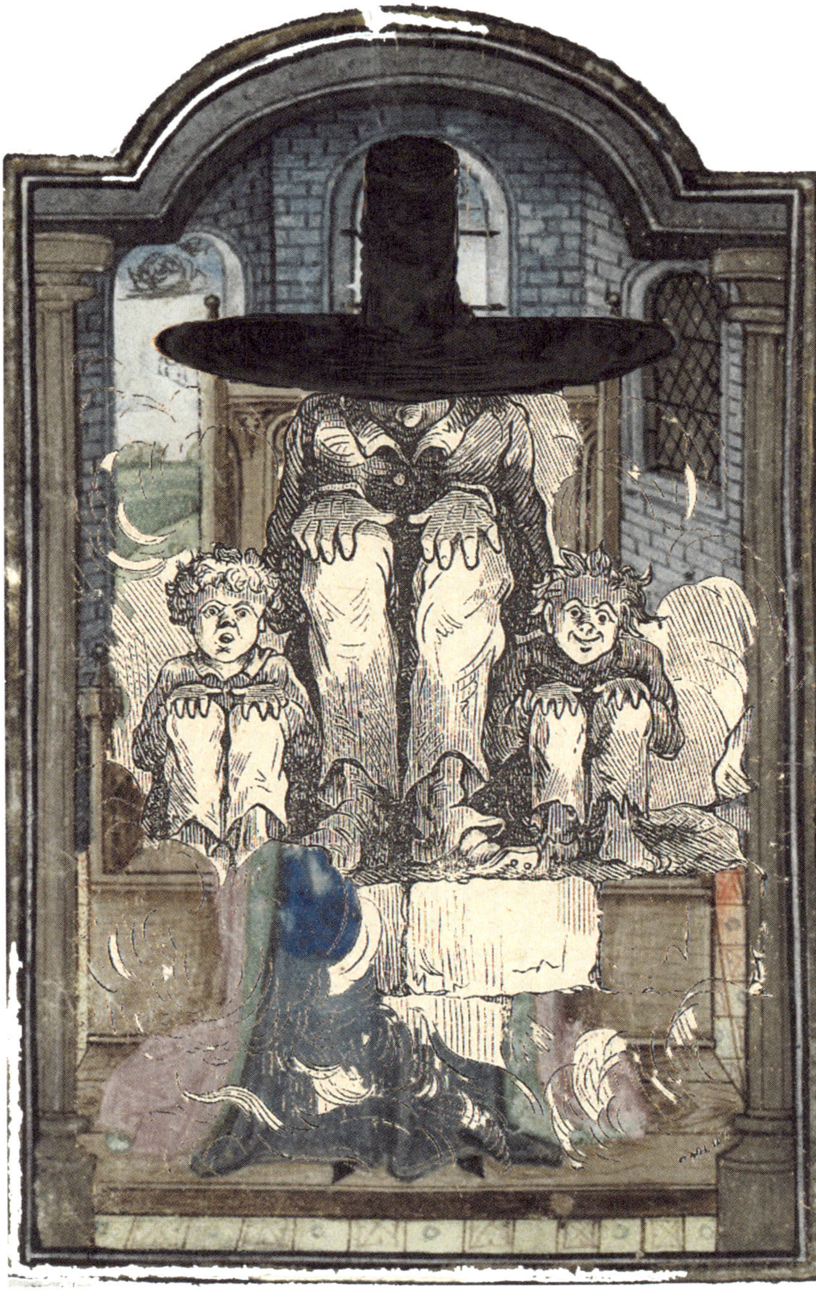

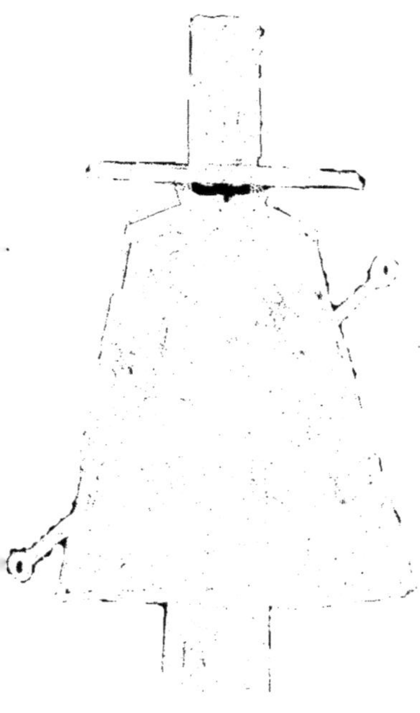

Matt, are you sleeping?
I'm trying.

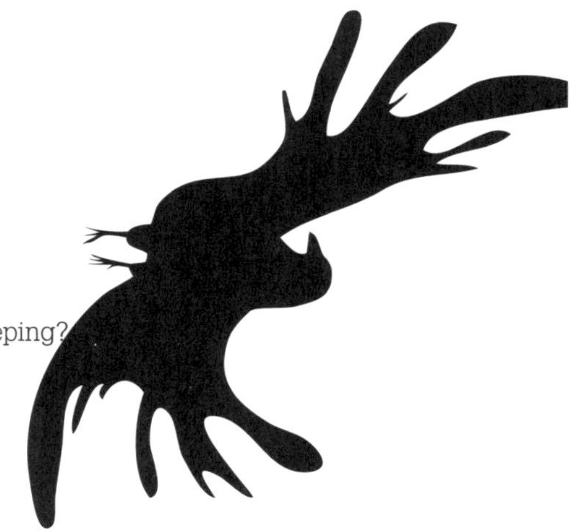

With the support of the Centre national des arts plastiques,
Ministère de la culture et de la Communication (research grant)

Translated
by Paul Buck & Catherine Petit

Specials Thanks to:
Juan Gimenez for his complicity

and to
Alain Robbe-Grillet
Alban Barré
Albéric Goudard
Captain Charles Johnson
Catherine Wood
Christian Hubert Delisle
Christophe Pérez
Christophe Penvert
Eungie Joo
Francis Alÿs
Franck Leibovici
Frédéric Bonnet
Gauthier Herrmann
Google
Grégoire Maisonneuve
Jane Faver
Jorge Luis Borges
Laure Limongi
Laurent Piron
Lubna Briand
Magali Guyon
Marcel Duchamp
Michel Blancsube
Philip K.Dick
Pierre Gaconnet.
Prue Lang
Samantha Theric
Séverine Quantin
Solal Guyon-Barré
Stanley Kubrick
Stephan May
Stéphane Corbinais
Stéphanie Delclos
Vanessa Desclaux
Yann Norry
Yuko Hasegawa

& all the pirates, smugglers and other miscreants of that Odyssey.

cover-images-scenario
Mathieu Briand (www.mathieubriand.com/)
fiction
Daniel Foucard (www.danielfoucard.net/)
comics
Juan Gimenez (www.juangimenez.com)
(pages 64-70-71-75-82-83-84-85-94)
from "A Matter of Time" (1982-1985), published by Catalan Communications, 1985

design
Lili Fleury
layout
Eleinad Ereivir
editor's assistant
Lise Revéret

THIS SERIES EDITED BY DANIELE RIVIERE

in the same series:
"School Spirit" by Pierre Huyghe & Douglas Coupland
"Spread Wide" by Kathy Acker, Paul Buck, John Cussans, Rebecca Stephens
"Life Extreme:an Illustrated Guide of New Life" by Eduardo Kac & Avital Ronell

1Cite Riverin
F-75010 PARIS
http://www.disvoir.com

ISBN: 9782914563369

PRINTED IN EUROPE
by
DZS GRAFIK
Slovenie
August 2008